A Kansas City
CHRISTMAS
Cookbook

D1405059

OOPS!

*While the authors
had visions of
sugarplums dancing
in their heads,
a pair of errors
crept into the recipe
for* Rudolph's
Nose Cookies
*(page 111) like
two bad mice:*

❧

In the ingredients,
use 1-3/4 cups
of flour (not 3/4 cup).

❧

In the instructions,
instead of "Drop by
teaspoonfuls
onto ungreased
baking sheets," the
directions should
read, "Place dough
balls on ungreased
baking sheets."

A Kansas City
CHRISTMAS
Cookbook

Karen Conde Adler

Jane Doyle Guthrie

TWO LANE PRESS

First printing October 1994

ISBN 1-878686-05-4

Printed in the United States of America

Cover design and lettering: Calvert Guthrie
Cover photo: Jenanne Jenkins

10 9 8 7 6 5 4 3 2 1 94 95 96 97 98

Two Lane Press
4245 Walnut Street
Kansas City, Missouri 64111
(816) 531-3119

To our parents

Robert and Denise Conde
John and Martha Doyle

For the wonderful Christmases past and to come

Contents

Acknowledgments

Kansas City's many traditions, cultures, and ethnic communities weave a rich holiday tapestry, and at the center of the celebrating are the treasured family foods of the season. The collection gathered in the pages that follow represents a wide range of winter customs, from hearty soups and baked goods laden with nuts and dried fruits to sizzling smoked turkeys and flaming desserts.

This book would not have been possible without the spirited support of the many friends and relatives who shared recipes with us. We are so grateful to Jill Adler, Ginny Beall, Jane Berkowitz, Daria Blankenship, Premila Borchardt, Shelley Bradley, Linda Buchner, Dee Conde, Richie Cusick, JoAnn Dodson, Marlene Doyle, Martha Doyle, Mary Ann Duckers, Carolyn Esberg, Judith Fertig, Jan Flanagan, Friends of Historic Fort Osage, Sarah Garney, Diane Garrett, Marcia Hamilton, Doris Hanks, Maraline Hayob, Dianne Hogerty, Brucie Hopkins, Ken Hornung, Susan Hornung, Janet Ida, Judy Jackson, Merrily Jackson, Susan Jackson, Glynda Jacobson, Bill Jeffreys, Vicki Johnson, Peggi Kilroy, Sheryl Koch, Georgia Lynch, Bobbi Marks, Nancy McKay, Caroline McKnight, J. J. Mirabile, Donna Missimer, Kay Moffatt, Dianne Morris, Cori Osburn, Gayle Parnow, Betsy Peterson, Diana Phillips, Debbie Pope, Deborah Reffitt, Jo Riley, Kim and Gil Rodriguez, Kelly Scanlon, Gladys Schwindler, Donna Smithmier, Mina Steen, Steve Stephenson, Angie Stout, Jean Tamburello, Lou Jane Temple, Judi Walker, Joanie Weaver, Carolyn Wells, Leslie Whitaker, Donna Wilting, Amy Winn, Bonnie Winston, The John Wornall House, Linda Yeates, Ellen Young, and Karen Zecy, for their generosity in helping us "build" this book. The spirit of Christmas is one of giving, and we found it here over and over.

Our thanks also go to Martie Eftink, Nancy McKay, and Sue Finucaine, for their valuable thoughts and comments as we developed the book. We are grateful, too, to Nancy Fuller, for her many hours of word processing and constant good cheer.

We extend our special appreciation to Mike Perkins and Linda Ray of Family Features. Their gracious service and attention to detail once again has made typesetting a pleasure rather than a chore.

Photographer Jenanne Jenkins opened her studio to us at a moment's notice and offered a beautiful selection of the Plaza in its winter splendor. We thank her sincerely for her many kindnesses.

Finally, we are most grateful to our husbands, Dick and Calvert, and to our very special families. From them came not just reserves of encouragement, but also the wonderful memories we drew on.

Christmas in Kansas City

"Five, four, three, two, one . . . " Every Thanksgiving night, like brilliant rippling dominos, the Plaza lights streak to life, borne on the roar of applause and a vast chorus of cheers. This event is certainly one of the most dramatic and well known of the Kansas City Christmas season, and it officially kicks off a calendar packed with fun for all ages and tastes.

Beyond the bounds of the Country Club Plaza, other parts of the city glow with holiday lights, too. Kansas Citians and revelers in surrounding areas can enjoy fairyland illuminations in many area parks and smaller shopping districts. Numerous historic sites and restored residences offer atmospheric candlelight tours, often accompanied by foods of the past and enthusiastic cadres of storytellers. Tree lightings comprise a category of their own; several exciting ones are staged in the area, such as the ceremony for the enormous Mayor's Christmas tree at Crown Center.

Annual tours and exhibits present an enjoyable option for a holiday afternoon or evening. Historic homes and village sites come alive for visitors via vintage decorations and reenactments. The Toy and Miniature Museum quite appropriately hosts an annual holiday exhibit—one year it might be teddy bears, another year crèches, another year trees. The Swope Park Greenhouse showcases a dazzling variety of poinsettias, and the J.C. Hall collection of decorated trees at the Hallmark Visitors Center offers many enchanting interpretations of a beloved holiday symbol. Numerous philanthropic and neighborhood organizations stage tours of beautifully decorated homes that inspire and delight those who visit.

Kansas Citians who thrill to live theater order tickets early for the Missouri Rep's annual "A Christmas Carol." Similarly, dance enthusiasts pirouette to the Midland each year for the fanciful, jubilant "Nutcracker." The Kansas City Symphony and many area orchestras offer numerous holiday concerts, and there's usually quite a selection of "Messiahs" to choose among, from the magnificent RLDS choir rendering to various informal singalongs. For pure fun, the annual "Merry Tuba Christmas" recital brings together over 275 of these gentle giants for an unusual holiday musicale.

Seasonal shopping opportunities abound here, many arranged as fund-raising events. The Junior League's Holiday Mart, the Gamma Phi Beta/KCPT Antiques & Garden Show, the Ladies of Charity Christmas Boutique, and the Dickens Holiday Fair, for instance, all present appealing and often extraordinary selections. Some of the holiday boutiques from philanthropic organizations operate in conjunction with homes tours, such as those sponsored by the Kappa Kappa Gamma alumnae. Many floral and decorating shops, as well as entire shopping districts, host open houses and displays of gorgeous ornaments, wreaths, garlands, tableware, and the like. Studio tours and sales such as those conducted by the Kansas City Clay Guild and the Art Institute provide access to one-of-a-kind items as well as contact with the artists who made them. The gift shops in area museums, from the Nelson-Atkins to Strawberry Hill, usually stock up with interesting, unusual items, often related to their own collections.

Much of the season's activity, of course, revolves around children. From the tony Ritz-Carlton to The Jones Store come teddy bear teas and breakfasts with Santa. Shopping centers create special play areas, elfin workshops, and seasonal displays like Gingerbread Lane. Historic sites such as the Lanesfield School offer children's crafts, customs, and games of Christmas Past. Santa arrives throughout the area by various entertaining modes—sleigh, helicopter, boat, even a Burlington Northern train—and the Fairy Princess takes her throne at the Kansas City Museum to listen to whispered Christmas lists. For those drawn to the outdoors, the Planetarium designs seasonal sky shows, ice skaters loop and glide at Crown Center, nature crafts get underway at Powell Gardens, and many Christmas tree farms offer extras such as hayrides and goodies to eat and drink. Children's centers such as Crittendon and the Ozanam Home usually put on Christmas events and holiday fundraisers such as movie premieres.

The spirit and ideals of the season often become most apparent in the activities of area churches and helping organizations. At the Cathedral of the Immaculate Conception, for example, visitors can become absorbed in over 150 nativity scenes from around the world, and many congregations also stage living nativity scenes and high-quality programs of religious music. The efforts of the Salvation Army, the Johnson County Christmas Bureau, the Marine Corps' Toys for Tots campaign, the Northland Christmas Store, and the Kansas City Community Kitchen at Grace & Holy Trinity Cathedral, for example, keep Kansas Citians aware of year-round needs in our community and offer many avenues for sharing during the holidays.

Kansas City is a special place to enjoy the holidays, as a visitor or as a resident. To keep up with holiday happenings, a wonderful source of information are the area convention and visitors bureaus. These organizations, along with chambers of commerce, parks and recreation departments, and area historical societies, usually publish annual brochures or calendars of events. Getting on their mailing lists ensures ongoing opportunities for educational and family activities.

Appetizers

Hors d'Oeuvres,
Dips, Spreads, & Beverages

Fiesta Pickled Shrimp

1 (2-pound) bag large, tail-on, peeled, deveined, and cooked
    frozen shrimp
2 large onions, sliced
7–8 bay leaves

MARINADE:
1-1/4 cups vegetable oil
3/4 cup white vinegar
1-1/2 teaspoons salt
2-1/2 teaspoons celery seed
2-1/2 tablespoons capers with liquid
Dash of Tabasco sauce

Alternate frozen shrimp and sliced onions with bay leaves in a
shallow glass baking dish. Mix all marinade ingredients and pour
over shrimp. Cover with foil and refrigerate for at least 36 hours
(48 if possible), spooning sauce over shrimp several times while
marinading. To serve, drain and mound onto a platter.

SERVES 8–10

The "cocktail buffet"
is a keystone of holiday
entertaining, and deciding
what to include can be like
a mouth-watering jigsaw
puzzle. Make space on the
table for these delicious
shrimp, which mosied in
from Merrily Jackson and
her Aunt Barbara in El
Paso, Texas. This zesty
combination looks as great
as it tastes.

Steamed Mussels

4 cloves garlic, minced
3 shallots, minced
2 tablespoons olive oil
1/2 cup chopped fresh parsley
1/4 teaspoon crushed red pepper flakes (or to taste)
3 pounds mussels, cleaned and bearded
3 cups dry white wine
Sourdough or garlic toasts

Sauté garlic and shallots in olive oil over medium heat until
translucent (about 5 minutes). Add parsley and pepper flakes, followed by mussels, then cover and increase heat to high. Cook for
3 minutes. Add wine and continue cooking, stirring occasionally
until the last mussel is open. Remove from heat (discard any mussels that did not open during cooking) and serve immediately
with sourdough or garlic toasts.

SERVES 4–6

For smaller groups,
consider delectable
mussels, such as these
from Bill Jeffreys. He also
recommends the following
variation: Transfer the
cooked mussels to a serving
bowl and reserve the
cooking liquid. Combine
1/2 cup cream and 2 tablespoons Pommery or Dijon-
style mustard with the
liquid, then cook the
mixture over high heat for
3 minutes. Pour over the
mussels and serve.

Maxine's Herring

For years radio personality Bobbi Marks has been telling Kansas Citians what's good to eat, and here she's provided her favorite recipe for herring, which her mother-in-law always served as an appetizer before Christmas dinner. Reach for these, too, when putting together a snack assortment to accompany wine or cocktails.

1 (4-pound) jar herring snacks
Juice of 1 lemon
2 white onions, sliced thinly
12 peppercorns
3 tablespoons firmly packed brown sugar
2 cups sour cream
2 tablespoons dry white wine
1/2 teaspoon ground cloves
Freshly ground pepper
Lemon slices and parsley sprigs
Cocktail rye slices

Rinse herring thoroughly (reserve jar), drain well in a colander, and place in a large bowl. Combine remaining ingredients and pour mixture over herring, stirring to cover well. Wash herring jar and return herring mixture to it, then close lid tightly and refrigerate. (Note: This is better made a few days in advance and keeps for several weeks.) When serving, grind a little fresh pepper over the top and garnish with lemon slices and parsley. Serve with cocktail rye slices.

SERVES 10–12

Crab Crostini

These crusty, chewy crostini offer guests a lively bite, courtesy of fresh ingredients that are available year-round. The crabmeat mixture can be made ahead and refrigerated; since assembly takes just a few minutes, you can put that off until close to serving time. Arrange the finished toasts on a platter lined with greens.

1/2 pound lump crabmeat, cleaned
1/2 cup diced red bell pepper
2 tablespoons plus 2 teaspoons reduced-calorie mayonnaise
2 tablespoons chopped fresh parsley
1 tablespoon chopped fresh chives
1 tablespoon fresh lime juice
1 tablespoon Dijon mustard
2 teaspoons freshly grated Parmesan cheese
4–5 drops Tabasco sauce
1/4 pound loaf Italian bread, cut into 16 slices

Preheat oven broiler, and lay a sheet of foil on a broiler pan. Combine crabmeat, bell pepper, mayonnaise, parsley, chives, lime juice, mustard, Parmesan, and Tabasco sauce, and blend well. Spread about 1 tablespoon of mixture on each slice of bread. Arrange slices on the broiler pan and broil 4 inches from heat for 5 to 6 minutes, or until lightly browned.

SERVES 6–8

Beef Tenderloin with Horseradish Sauce

1 (5- to 6-pound) beef tenderloin
2 (16-ounce) bottles zesty Italian salad dressing
1/3 cup Allegro meat and vegetable marinade
1/3 cup Burgundy wine
1 teaspoon soy sauce
1 clove garlic, minced
1/2 teaspoon lemon pepper
French bread slices

SAUCE:
1 cup mayonnaise
1-1/2 tablespoons prepared horseradish

Combine sauce ingredients and refrigerate, tightly covered, until ready to serve. Place meat in a large glass baking dish or heavy-duty resealable plastic bag. Combine salad dressing, marinade, wine, soy sauce, garlic, and lemon pepper, and pour over meat. Cover and refrigerate for 8 hours, turning occasionally. Drain meat and discard marinade. Cook on a covered grill over high heat for 3 minutes, then turn and grill for 3 minutes more. Reduce heat to low and continue to cook covered for 12 minutes, or until a meat thermometer inserted into the thickest portion registers 140 degrees (rare). Let meat stand for 15 minutes before slicing. Serve with sauce and sliced French bread.

SERVES 20–24

Peggi Kilroy offers this succulent beef tenderloin as an appetizer, but it would also serve well as the centerpiece to a holiday meal. She warns that it's so good, it's worth fighting through two feet of snow to get to it!

Wild Duck Rumaki

2 whole boneless, skinless duck breasts, cubed
2 cups milk
1 pound sliced bacon, halved

In a covered container, marinate cubed meat in milk overnight in the refrigerator. Preheat oven broiler. Discard milk and wrap each cube in a half slice of bacon, securing with a water-soaked toothpick. Broil for 30 minutes (turning once) or until bacon is crisp. Serve hot.

SERVES 8–10

Wild game also adds a twist to a buffet. Anyone who picks up one of these rumaki expecting a chicken liver or a water chestnut is in for a delightful surprise. Besides tasting ever so good, these little brochettes offer a clever way to stretch duck meat for a crowd.

Aunt Louise's Chopped Chicken Salad

This chunky chicken salad from Glynda Jacobson makes a delicious old-fashioned appetizer, but it also holds up its end on a spread of hors d'oeuvres when surrounded by squares of sweet and savory breads. Don't make the mistake of substituting mayonnaise for the Miracle Whip; the latter is the "secret ingredient."

4 cups coarsely chopped cooked chicken (white and dark meat)
2 cups coarsely chopped celery
1 cup chopped white onion
1-1/2 cups coarsely chopped English walnuts
1 cup Miracle Whip (no substitutions)
2 tablespoons sugar
1 teaspoon white vinegar
Salt and pepper to taste
Garlic powder to taste
Cocktail rye and date nut bread slices

Combine chicken, celery, onion, and walnuts, and set aside. Thoroughly combine Miracle Whip, sugar, vinegar, salt, pepper, and garlic powder, and toss with chicken mixture. Cover and refrigerate. Serve chilled with cocktail rye and small squares of date nut bread.

SERVES 12–16

Pork Tenderloin with Mustard Sauce

Sliced pork tenderloins also serve as reliably popular hors d'oeuvres. You can grill or broil this succulent version instead of roasting if you prefer—just make sure there's plenty for everyone. In the unlikely event of leftovers, the meat and sauce make a delicious sandwich paired with sliced onions and pickles on a hard roll.

2 (3/4-pound) pork tenderloins
2 tablespoons firmly packed brown sugar
1/4 cup soy sauce
1/3 cup dry red wine

SAUCE:
1/2 cup catsup
1 tablespoon dry mustard
1 tablespoon cider vinegar
1/2 teaspoon curry powder

Combine sauce ingredients and refrigerate, tightly covered, until ready to serve. In a glass baking dish, combine sugar, soy sauce, and wine. Add tenderloins, cover, and marinate in refrigerator for 1 to 2 hours. Preheat oven to 350 degrees. Remove tenderloins from marinade (reserve liquid) and roast for about 1 hour, basting 4 or 5 times with reserved marinade. When tenderloins are cool, cut diagonally into thin slices and serve with sauce.

SERVES 8–10

Sweet & Sour Smokies

2/3 cup firmly packed brown sugar
2 tablespoons cornstarch
2 teaspoons dry mustard
2/3 cup cider vinegar
1 cup undrained crushed pineapple
1/2 cup catsup
1/2 cup water
1/4 cup finely chopped onion
2 tablespoons soy sauce
Salt and pepper to taste
1 (16-ounce) package small smoked sausages

In a medium saucepan, combine first 9 ingredients and simmer over medium heat until smooth and glossy, stirring constantly. Stir in salt and pepper, then add sausages and heat thoroughly. Keep warm in a chafing dish and provide cocktail picks to serve. (Note: This sauce also works well for meatballs or spareribs.)

SERVES 6–8

When Jan Flanagan fixes these flavorful little sausages, her husband and boys know it's the first Sunday in December and time to trim the tree. These go well with other informal buffet items—a relish tray, cold spiced shrimp, smoked cheese and crackers, apple and pear slices, and an assortment of Christmas cookies.

Holiday Pâté

1 pound chicken livers
1 cup chicken broth
1/4 medium onion, sliced
2 tablespoons plus 2 teaspoons dried rosemary
6 slices bacon, fried and crumbled
1/2 cup (1 stick) butter, softened
1/2 teaspoon dry mustard
1/4 teaspoon salt
1/8 teaspoon pepper
1 jar peperoncini peppers, drained
Rye crackers

Simmer chicken livers in broth with onion and rosemary until tender (about 15 minutes). Cool, drain, and reserve 1/4 cup cooking liquid. Place reserved cooking liquid, livers, onions, rosemary, bacon crumbles, butter, mustard, salt, and pepper into a food processor and whirl until smooth. Refrigerate in a covered container overnight to blend flavors. Serve with rye crackers and peperoncini peppers.

SERVES 6–8

Similarly, a linchpin holiday treat at the home of Georgia and Jim Lynch is this scrumptious spiced pâté. The bite of the peperoncini peppers is essential to fully enjoying this creation, which shows up like Santa every Christmas Eve at the Lynchs'.

Sign of Welcome Pâté

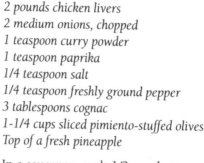

The gracious presentation of Dianne Hogerty's pâté in the shape of a pineapple (the traditional sign of welcome) offers a spectacular centerpiece for a buffet, but creating the "pineapple" actually requires very little effort. Since you can make it a week ahead (or longer, and then freeze), preparing this special appetizer during the busy holiday season is very "doable."

2 cups (4 sticks) butter, softened
2 pounds chicken livers
2 medium onions, chopped
1 teaspoon curry powder
1 teaspoon paprika
1/4 teaspoon salt
1/4 teaspoon freshly ground pepper
3 tablespoons cognac
1-1/4 cups sliced pimiento-stuffed olives
Top of a fresh pineapple

In a saucepan, melt 1/2 cup butter and add chicken livers, onions, curry powder, paprika, salt, and pepper. Cover and cook until livers are no longer pink (about 8 minutes). Whirl mixture little by little in a blender or food processor until smooth. Transfer mixture to a bowl and stir in remaining butter and cognac, blending well. Refrigerate until mixture may be molded (at least 3 hours). On a serving platter, mold liver mixture into an upright pineapple shape. Starting at the base of the molded mixture, press sliced olives in rows encircling the pâté so that it is completely covered except the very top. Cap with the fresh pineapple top before serving. (Note: To freeze, wrap entire mold in plastic wrap and then foil, sealing securely. Remove 24 hours before serving and thaw in refrigerator.)

SERVES 30–40

Caviar and Avocado Mold

The green rim of avocado surrounding glistening caviar also offers an appealing presentation. Pairing a combination of red and black caviar, either side by side or in a four-square pattern, lends an elegant look to a very simple combination of elements.

Pulp from 2 large ripe avocados
1/2 cup sour cream, whipped
1-1/2 tablespoons fresh lime juice
1/4 teaspoon salt (or to taste)
1/2 cup red or black caviar (or 1/4 cup of each)
Crackers, toasts, or tortilla chips

Thoroughly mash avocado pulp, then stir in sour cream, lime juice, and salt until blended. Spoon evenly into a serving bowl. Using the back of a spoon, carefully make a cavity in the center of the avocado mixture and then spoon in caviar (if using red and black caviar, spoon in side by side). Cover and refrigerate. Serve with crackers, toasts, or tortilla chips.

SERVES 8–10

Salmon Cheesecake

1 cup crushed buttery crackers
3 tablespoons butter, melted
2 (8-ounce) packages cream cheese, softened
3 eggs
3/4 cup sour cream
1/2 teaspoon fresh lemon juice
1 (7-3/4-ounce) can salmon, cleaned, drained, and flaked
2 tablespoons grated onion
White pepper to taste
Assorted crackers

Preheat oven to 350 degrees. Combine butter and cracker crumbs, and press into an 8-inch springform pan. Bake for 10 minutes, then remove and reduce oven temperature to 325 degrees. Combine cream cheese, eggs, and 1/4 cup sour cream, beating until smooth. Stir in lemon juice, flaked salmon, onion, and pepper. Pour mixture into prepared crust and bake for 45 to 50 minutes. Cool and top with remaining 1/2 cup sour cream. Refrigerate until ready to serve. Serve with crackers.

SERVES 16–20

Savory cheesecakes feed a crowd and garnish beautifully for an open house or party buffet. This one is a favorite of Dianne Morris, who creates a wreath of chopped parsley on the sour cream surface and then adds red bell pepper pieces to look like berries or other decorations. You can make this 3 days ahead, and leftovers freeze well.

Feta Cheesecake

2-1/2 cups toasted bread crumbs
3/4 cup melted butter
12 ounces feta cheese
12 ounces cream cheese
2 cups sour cream
2 eggs
1-1/2 teaspoons dried basil or fines herbes
Pepper to taste

Preheat oven to 325 degrees. Combine butter and bread crumbs, and press into a 12-inch springform pan. Whirl cheeses, sour cream, eggs, basil, and pepper in a food processor and pour mixture into prepared crust. Bake for 20 to 25 minutes. Cover and chill overnight. Serve at room temperature with unsalted crackers. (Note: Recipe can be halved and prepared in an 8-inch springform pan. Freezes well.)

SERVES 20–30

Karen Zecy learned to make this sublime feta cheesecake in one of Linda Davis's cooking classes. Karen's husband is of Greek heritage, so tangy feta is a favored staple in their household. Karen says she covers the bottom of the pan with foil before pressing in the crust, so that after baking she can easily slip the cooled cheesecake onto a serving platter.

Southwestern Cheesecake

The distinctive tastes of the Southwest have become familiar favorites whenever and wherever friends gather, and this cheesecake from Susan Hornung appealingly showcases this very popular family of flavors. The recipe can be made a day ahead, and the consistency allows spreading easily onto tortilla chips as well as crackers or toasts.

2 (8-ounce) packages cream cheese, softened
8 ounces grated sharp cheddar cheese
1 (1-1/4-ounce) package taco seasoning
2 cups sour cream
3 eggs
1 (4-ounce) can diced green chilies, drained
1/2 cup diced red bell pepper
1/2 cup mild salsa (or hot, to taste)
1 (6-ounce) carton frozen avocado dip
2 tomatoes, seeded and diced
Tortilla chips

Preheat oven to 350 degrees. Beat together cheeses and taco seasoning until mixture becomes fluffy. Stir in 1 cup sour cream. Beat in eggs 1 at a time, blending well. Fold in chilies and bell pepper. Pour mixture into a 9-inch springform pan and bake until center is almost firm (about 40 to 45 minutes; don't overbake—it firms as it cools). Cool on rack for 10 minutes. Combine remaining sour cream with salsa and spread on top of cheesecake. Return to oven for 7 to 8 minutes. Cool on rack for 30 minutes, then refrigerate in springform pan for several hours or overnight. To serve, transfer to a platter, spread with avocado dip, and top with diced tomatoes. Serve with tortilla chips.

SERVES 20–24

Holiday Torta

The torta also offers an attractive "package" for a party cheese spread. Joanie Weaver supplied this one, which looks particularly pretty at holiday festivities because of its layers of red and green and white.

2 (8-ounce) packages light cream cheese, softened
1 package Hidden Valley Ranch Original Ranch salad dressing
1 (6-ounce) jar marinated artichoke hearts, drained and chopped
3 tablespoons minced fresh parsley, plus additional to garnish
1/2 red bell pepper, chopped, plus additional to garnish
Pita toasts or crackers

Cream together cheese and salad dressing mix. In a separate bowl, stir together artichokes, parsley, and bell pepper. In a 3-cup bowl lined with plastic wrap, alternate layers of cheese and vegetable mixtures, beginning and ending with a cheese layer (3 cheese layers, 2 vegetable layers). Refrigerate for 4 hours or overnight. Invert onto a serving plate and remove plastic wrap. Garnish top with a bell pepper cutout (such as a star) and minced parsley. Serve with pita toasts and crackers.

SERVES 10–12

Torta Primavera

24 prepared crêpes
1-1/2 pounds fresh spinach
3 tablespoons butter, melted
2 cloves garlic, crushed
Salt and pepper to taste
Mayonnaise
3/4 pound Genoa salami, sliced paper thin
12 ounces provolone cheese, sliced paper thin
5 hard-cooked eggs, sliced paper thin
3/4 pound smoked or baked ham, sliced paper thin

Sauté spinach in butter seasoned with garlic, salt, and pepper. Cool to room temperature (or refrigerate for later assembly). To assemble, spread 1 crêpe with a light coat of mayonnaise and top with a layer of each filling (salami, provolone, eggs, ham, and spinach). Continue layering in this way (spreading both sides of subsequent crêpes with mayonnaise to hold torta together) and finish with a crêpe. Anchor with long toothpicks if necessary. "Ice" the top crêpe with mayonnaise and decorate in holiday colors (such as cherry tomato rosettes with parsley stems and leaves). Refrigerate to set (can be made a day ahead), then slice into thin wedges to serve.

SERVES 20–30

Jean Tamburello of Marty's Bar-B-Q in the Northland doesn't have to think twice about what's her favorite holiday appetizer. In fact, this torta was one of her grandfather's favorites, too. Although preparation and assembly are time-consuming (particularly if you make your own crêpes), the payoff is great in terms of taste and presentation. This can be made a day ahead and refrigerated, as well as halved for smaller crowds.

Smoky Cheddar-Beef Ball

6 ounces sharp cheddar cheese, grated finely
2 (8-ounce) packages cream cheese, softened
1 small onion, chopped
1 teaspoon Worcestershire sauce
1/8 teaspoon garlic powder
Liquid smoke to taste
1–2 (2-1/4-ounce) packages Armour dried beef, chopped finely
Milk
Crackers or toasts

Combine cheeses, onion, Worcestershire sauce, garlic powder, liquid smoke, and 1/2 cup chopped dried beef. Add milk a little at a time to smooth mixture as needed. Refrigerate until firm. Shape chilled mixture into a ball and roll in additional chopped dried beef until thoroughly coated. Cover and refrigerate again, then bring to room temperature when ready to serve. Serve with firm crackers or toasts.

SERVES 16–20

Cheeseballs are also longtime traditional favorites. Made well ahead, then wrapped tightly and kept cold, they make appealing gifts for friends and neighbors as well as on-hand, spur-of-the-moment refreshments for drop-in holiday guests or carolers. This one's rich smoky taste is a guaranteed crowd pleaser.

Curried Chutney Cheese Spread

Rich chutneys and fragrant spices pair deliciously in all manner of holiday foods. Although this calls for traditional Major Grey's, a variety of chutneys would work well—experiment with a homemade version.

1 (8-ounce) package Neufchâtel cheese, softened
1/2 cup Major Grey's chutney, chopped finely
1 teaspoon curry powder
1/4 teaspoon dry mustard
1 small onion, chopped
1/2 cup chopped toasted pecans
Garlic-flavored pita or bagel crisps

Combine cheese, chutney, spices, and onion, spoon into a crock or serving bowl, and then top with toasted pecans. Serve with garlic pita crisps or bagel crisps.

SERVES 8–10

Spanakopitas

Guests will enjoy their cheese "gift wrapped," too. These Greek phyllo parcels from Karen Zecy freeze well, and the recipe yields enough for more than one party. The secret to success in working with these tissue-thin layers of pastry is to keep them covered and moist until brushed with butter during filling.

4 (10-ounce) packages frozen chopped spinach, thawed and
    squeezed dry
1 (8-ounce) package cream cheese, softened
16 ounces feta cheese, crumbled
1/2 cup grated Romano cheese
4 eggs, beaten
1 small onion, minced
3 tablespoons olive oil
1 teaspoon dill weed, minced
1 teaspoon ground nutmeg
1 teaspoon salt
1/4 teaspoon pepper
4 (16-ounce) packages frozen phyllo, thawed
4 cups (8 sticks) butter, melted

Combine first 11 ingredients to form filling mixture and set aside. Cut stacked phyllo sheets from each package in half, forming 7-by-18-inch strips. (Keep sheets covered at all times with plastic wrap or a damp towel.) To fill sheets, work with 7-inch side parallel to edge of work surface. One strip at a time, brush phyllo with butter and spoon 1 tablespoon of filling near bottom of strip. Fold up bottom edge to cover filling, then fold in left and right sides, top to bottom, forming a narrow vertical strip about 2 inches wide. Brush phyllo again with butter. Like folding a flag, start with a bottom corner of the strip and fold up and over, again and again, to create a triangular packet. Brush finished triangles with butter to seal and arrange in squares on baking sheets (preferably aluminum). Cover and freeze. Preheat oven to 350 degrees. Bake frozen triangles for 20 to 25 minutes. Serve hot.

MAKES 160 TRIANGLES

Liptauer Dip

1 (8-ounce) carton nonfat plain yogurt, frozen then thawed
1 (8-ounce) carton low-fat cottage cheese or part-skim ricotta
1 tablespoon Hungarian paprika
1 tablespoon caraway seed
1 teaspoon grated onion
1/4 cup small capers (drained)
2 tablespoons minced fresh chives or scallions
Dash of tamari sauce
Salt and white pepper to taste
Assorted raw vegetables

Pour thawed yogurt into a sieve lined with cheesecloth and let drain for 1 hour. Transfer yogurt to a blender or food processor, add cottage cheese, and whirl until smooth. Pour into a small bowl and stir in remaining ingredients. Cover and refrigerate overnight. Serve with assorted raw vegetables.

MAKES ABOUT 2 CUPS

Reddened by the paprika, this dip looks very pretty in the center of a crudité wreath. Insert toothpicks into the bottoms of colorful raw vegetable "dippers"— green broccoli florets, red cherry tomatoes, white cauliflower pieces, and so forth—and stick them into a lettuce-wrapped styrofoam wreath, taking care to produce a background of shades of green, interspersed with "ornaments" of other colors.

Garlic-Anchovy Pizza

1 (12-inch) loaf focaccia (or prepared pizza crust)
1/4 cup olive oil
8 cloves garlic, minced
20 anchovy fillets, rinsed, patted dry, and minced
2 tablespoons fresh lemon juice
Freshly ground pink, green, and black pepper to taste

Preheat oven to 325 degrees. Heat oil, then add garlic and sauté until soft (do not brown). Add anchovies to pan and stir constantly until mixture becomes a paste. Stir in lemon juice and peppers. Spread warm paste evenly over focaccia and place in the oven until warmed through. Cut into small wedges or squares to serve. (Note: If starting with unbaked pizza crust, bake almost completely first before spreading with anchovy paste and returning to oven.)

SERVES 6–8

Delicious focaccia also serves as a versatile "canvas" for many different party spreads and toppings. This recipe could also be a tasty accompaniment to a hearty Italian-style soup.

Spicy Shrimp Dip

This shrimp dip is an adaptation of the enormously popular version served at the S&D Oyster Company restaurant in Dallas. Although the recipe produces a Texas-size portion, perfect for a large gathering or open house, it does cut back well for smaller crowds.

2 pounds frozen, precooked shrimp, thawed
1 (8-ounce) package cream cheese, softened
1/2 cup mayonnaise
1 cup Thousand Island dressing
1/4 cup minced green onions (white and green parts)
1 small onion, grated
4 teaspoons Tabasco sauce
1 tablespoon seasoned salt
1 tablespoon prepared horseradish
Assorted crackers or toasts

Finely chop shrimp and set aside. Blend cream cheese with mayonnaise and dressing. Stir in shrimp, onion, Tabasco sauce, seasoned salt, and horseradish. Adjust seasonings to taste, then refrigerate until ready to serve. Serve with crackers or toasts. (Note: Recipe may be halved and/or refrigerated overnight.)

MAKES ABOUT 6 CUPS

Green Chili Artichoke Dip

Also an out-of-towner, this artichoke dip shared by Betsy Peterson originated with Susie Magrino, owner of Charity's Restaurant in Frisco, Colorado. The pale green artichokes alongside the red pimientos offer a subtle holiday palette, and served warm, this is the perfect offering after an ice skating party or a trip to the Christmas tree farm.

2 (4-ounce) cans chopped green chilies
2 (14-ounce) cans artichoke hearts, drained and quartered
1 cup mayonnaise
1 cup freshly grated Parmesan cheese
1 (2-ounce) jar pimientos, drained
Toasts or tortilla chips

Preheat oven to 350 degrees. Combine all ingredients in an oven-proof container and heat for 30 minutes. Serve warm with toasts or tortilla chips.

MAKES ABOUT 3 CUPS

Fried Pasta with Marinara Sauce

1/2 cup freshly grated Parmesan cheese
1/4 cup Italian-style bread crumbs
3 cups olive oil
8 ounces tricolor rotini pasta, cooked al dente and cooled
1 cup marinara sauce, warmed

Combine cheese and bread crumbs, and set aside. Heat olive oil to 350 degrees and deep-fry cooked pasta in small batches for about 4 minutes, or until crunchy and lightly browned. Remove from oil with a slotted spoon and drain on paper towels. Place pasta in a bowl with Parmesan cheese–bread crumb mixture and toss lightly to coat. Serve immediately with warm marinara sauce as a dip.

SERVES 8–10

The red, green, and white rotini can be mounded around the bowl of red marinara sauce, offering a festive look anytime during the holidays. Since this serves best while still warm, fix it for small groups when you're just putting out a few things to munch on— it's a wonderful snack for watching "It's a Wonderful Life."

Cheese Straws

1/2 cup (1 stick) butter, softened
1-1/2 cups all-purpose flour
1-1/2 teaspoons baking powder
1 teaspoon salt
1/2 teaspoon cayenne pepper
2-1/4 cups grated sharp cheddar cheese

Preheat oven to 350 degrees. Combine butter with dry ingredients (mixture is crumbly, so work with hands), then add cheese and mix well. Roll dough on a lightly floured surface until about 1/8-inch thick. Run fork tines along dough to make a streaked pattern, then cut into 1/2-by-2-inch strips. Place on an ungreased nonstick baking sheet and bake for 10 to 12 minutes or until lightly browned. Store in an airtight container or freeze until ready to serve. (Note: Best if made a day ahead.)

MAKES SEVERAL DOZEN

For parties large and small, these traditional cheese straws from Carolyn Esberg are the perfect "pick up" food. On a bounteous cocktail buffet or with fruit slices and a glass of wine, these always fit in with your party plans. Keep plenty in the freezer from November to January!

Sweet and Spicy Coated Pecans

Though widely available (and affordable) now, nuts were once hoarded for just the most special occasions, and thus showed up in Christmas stockings and in holiday recipes as a sign of seasonal celebrating. Nutmeats combine well with a variety of flavors—sugary and sweet, as in Marlene Doyle's coated pecans, or hot and savory, such as with the deviled cashews that follow. Though perhaps more commonplace today, nuts still make much-appreciated gifts. If you prefer, instead of flavoring them, try just preparing a roasted mix of shelled walnuts, almonds, pecans, sunflower seeds, pumpkin seeds, and cashews. Roast the combination at 350 degrees in a large pan for about 20 minutes. When cool, add raisins and toss well. The mix stores beautifully in decorated airtight containers and tins.

1 pound pecans
1 tablespoon ground cinnamon
1 teaspoon ground nutmeg
1 cup sugar
1 egg white
1 tablespoon water

Preheat oven to 300 degrees. Combine cinnamon, nutmeg, and sugar, and set aside. Beat egg white and water until foamy, then add pecans and toss until coated well. Roll pecans in spice mix, then transfer to a baking sheet and bake for 35 minutes, stirring and turning over every 10 minutes. When cool, store in an airtight container.

MAKES ABOUT 4 CUPS

Rosemary Walnuts

2 cups English walnuts
2-1/2 tablespoons butter
2 teaspoons crushed dried rosemary
1 teaspoon salt
1/2 teaspoon cayenne (or to taste)

Preheat oven to 350 degrees. Melt butter and add crushed rosemary, salt, and cayenne. Pour mixture over walnuts and toss to coat. Spread nuts on a baking sheet and bake for 10 minutes. When cool, store in an airtight container.

MAKES 2 CUPS

Deviled Cashews

2 cups unsalted cashews
1-1/2 tablespoons butter or margarine
1 teaspoon salt
1/4 teaspoon cayenne pepper
1/2 teaspoon ground cumin
1/2 teaspoon ground coriander

Sauté cashews in butter until golden (about 3 minutes). Drain. Combine salt and spices, then toss with nuts. When cool, store in an airtight container.

MAKES 2 CUPS

Sesame and Five-Spice Almonds

2 cups whole unsalted almonds
2 teaspoons vegetable oil
2 teaspoons sesame oil
1 teaspoon Chinese five spice
Salt to taste

Preheat oven to 350 degrees. Spread nuts in a shallow baking pan and toast, uncovered, for 8 to 10 minutes or until golden, stirring often. Drizzle with oils, then stir in spice and salt, tossing to coat. Return to oven for 2 to 3 minutes more, stirring often. Let stand, uncovered, for about 5 minutes to crisp. When cool, store in an airtight container.

MAKES 2 CUPS

Curried Popcorn

8–10 cups popped popcorn
1/3 cup melted butter or margarine
1 teaspoon curry powder
Salt to taste

Combine melted butter with curry powder and salt, then toss gently but thoroughly with popcorn. Store in an airtight container.

SERVES 6–8

Garlic-Cheese Popcorn

8 cups warm popped popcorn
1/3 cup grated Romano cheese
1/3 cup grated Parmesan cheese
2 teaspoons salt
1 teaspoon garlic powder
1 teaspoon onion powder

Combine cheeses and seasonings well, then toss gently but thoroughly with warm popcorn. Serve immediately.

SERVES 4–6

Popcorn is also a traditional sign of the holidays, mounded in bowls for eating as well as strung on garlands for decorating. Making and tinting popcorn balls is also a favorite tradition in many households, and Mina Steen and her children always place some of the pretty colored balls on the mantel. For informal entertaining, pop enough corn (maybe in the fireplace?) to flavor several ways for guests' tastes. Just as with nuts, the warm taste of corn marries well with many different coatings—caramel, cinnamon, herbed, cheesy, spicy, whatever you fancy.

Meme's Kentucky Eggnog

6 quarts commercial eggnog (dairy variety, not canned)
3 quarts half-and-half
Nutmeg to taste
1/2 gallon good-quality vanilla ice cream
1-1/2 to 2 cups premium-label Kentucky bourbon
1 cup white rum
4–6 egg whites

In a large punchbowl, combine eggnog and half-and-half, add a good sprinkling of nutmeg, and stir well. Add ice cream to mixture in large scoops, followed by bourbon, rum, and additional nutmeg to taste, stirring gently so as not to break up or melt ice cream. Beat egg whites until stiff and spoon over top of mixture. Garnish with additional nutmeg and serve.

SERVES 30–40

Wornall House Wassail

4 quarts water
4 cinnamon sticks
2 teaspoons whole cloves (or to taste)
1 cup sugar
1 (6-ounce) can orange juice concentrate
1/2 cup fresh lemon juice
8–9 tea bags

Combine water, cinnamon sticks, and cloves, and bring to a boil. Remove from heat and add remaining ingredients. Cover and let steep for 10 minutes. Remove tea bags and serve immediately.

SERVES 30–36

Certain beverages are a must at the holidays, among them eggnog and English wassail. As one is cold and one hot, one is spiked and one not, this pair offers an inviting selection for a variety of Yuletide gatherings. Frances ("Meme") Doyle's eggnog always was (and still is, thanks to Aunt Marlene) as eagerly awaited as St. Nick himself. The secret to its smooth, smooth taste is plenty of delicious ice cream and a dose of very good Kentucky bourbon. The warm wassail that follows is an annual delight from the historic John Wornall House in Brookside, shared with visitors during the festive candlelight tours of the beautiful home.

Entrees

Meats, Pasta,
Soups, & Brunch

Golden Christmas Goose

1 (10- to 12-pound) goose
Salt and pepper to taste
1/2 cup vegetable oil
1 cup dry white wine
1 cup wine sauce (recipe follows)
3 carrots, sliced
3 stalks celery, sliced
1 onion, chunked
2 cloves garlic, chopped

SAUCE:
2 strips bacon
3–4 carrots, sliced
1 onion, chopped
2 teaspoons dried thyme
2 bay leaves
Pepper to taste
1/3 cup butter or margarine
1-1/4 cups all-purpose flour
3 (14-1/2-ounce) cans beef broth
2–3 tomatoes, peeled and coarsely chopped
1 cup dry white wine

The day before serving, begin preparation of sauce. Sauté bacon until crisp, then drain and crumble. To drippings remaining in pan, add carrots, onion, thyme, bay leaves, pepper, and bacon pieces. Add butter and melt. Slowly stir in flour to form a roux, then stir in 2 cans beef broth, smoothing out any lumps that form. Simmer uncovered over very low heat for 3 hours, then remove from heat and refrigerate overnight. Return sauce to heat and add remaining can of broth, tomatoes, and white wine. Simmer over very low heat for 2 hours, then refrigerate again if not serving immediately.

Rinse goose well, pat dry, and season skin and cavity with salt and pepper. Truss if desired. Heat vegetable oil and brown goose well on all sides, turning several times (this releases grease from bird). Preheat oven to 325 degrees. Arrange neck and giblets around base of goose in roasting pan, then pour white wine and 1 cup wine sauce over bird. Over and around goose, sprinkle carrots, celery, onion, and garlic. Cover and roast for 3 to 3-1/2 hours. Every 30 minutes, baste well. As grease rises in pan, skim off thoroughly. Uncover during last 30 minutes to brown. Goose is done when legs move easily. Serve with roasted vegetables and warm wine sauce.

SERVES 6

Although fans of horror novelist Richie Tankersley Cusick might expect to sup on gothic goose with terrifying trimmings, her Lenexa parlor hosts only the kindliest gatherings at Christmastime. One of these is an annual dinner for several longtime chums, where the main attraction is this delicious bird and savory wine sauce. Although goose has a reputation for being greasy, this version is not; frequently skimming off the fat, however, is absolutely essential.

Wornall House Roast Duckling

Kay Moffat of the Wornall House shared this very traditional 1800s-style recipe for roast duck, which appeared years ago in The Kansas City Star. Fresh domestic duck is often not available year-round; about 90 percent of ducks that appear on the market are frozen. Thaw frozen birds in the refrigerator, allowing roughly 24 to 36 hours (depending on the size of the duck).

1 (4- to 5-pound) duckling
1-1/4 teaspoons pepper
2 teaspoons salt
1/2 teaspoon cayenne pepper
1/2 teaspoon dried thyme

Preheat oven to 475 degrees. Rinse duck and pat dry. Season cavity with 3/4 teaspoon pepper, 3/4 teaspoon salt, 1/4 teaspoon cayenne pepper, and thyme. Sprinkle remaining salt and peppers on outside of bird, then prick skin with a roasting fork. Roast duck uncovered for 20 minutes, then reduce heat to 350 degrees, cover, and roast for 80 minutes more, basting frequently with pan drippings. Increase heat to 475 degrees and roast uncovered for 20 minutes to crisp. Remove from pan to drain fat. Cool slightly before carving.

SERVES 4

Roasted Turkey Asia

Though this unusual recipe for turkey is anything but traditional, Diana Phillips maintains it's the juiciest bird she's ever prepared. Guests won't miss the fact that there's no gravy or stuffing with this one—they'll enjoy the extra room for dessert.

1 fresh turkey (size depends on number to serve)
4 teaspoons salt
4 stalks celery
6 green onions
6 slices fresh ginger
2 dried star anise pods
6 cloves garlic
2 teaspoons ground turmeric
4 dried orange peel slices
2 medium yellow onions, quartered
3 teaspoons peanut oil
12 cups water

The day before cooking, cover turkey with salt and refrigerate, covered, for 6 to 8 hours. Rinse turkey thoroughly and pat dry. Cover with aluminum foil and place in a cool, dry place overnight. Preheat oven to 450 degrees. Evenly space celery stalks in bottom of roasting pan. Sit turkey on celery, then put green onions, 2 slices ginger, 1 crumbled star anise, and 2 cloves garlic into cavity. Rub turmeric on top, and surround turkey with remaining ginger, garlic, anise, orange peel, and onions. Roast for 45 minutes, then turn bird over and roast for 30 minutes more. Turn again and coat top with peanut oil. Add water to pan, reduce heat to 400 degrees, and roast for 30 minutes more, or until golden. Let stand for 15 minutes out of pan before carving.

SERVINGS VARY BY SIZE OF BIRD

Apple-Smoked Turkey Breast

1 (8- to 10-pound) turkey breast (bone-in)
2 cups balsamic vinegar
1/4 cup water
1/4 cup sea salt
3 tablespoons chili powder
2 tablespoons pepper
1/4 teaspoon dried marjoram
1/4 teaspoon dried lemon peel

Combine vinegar, water, salt, chili powder, pepper, marjoram, and lemon peel, and whirl for 3 minutes in a blender or food processor. Transfer to a nonmetal container and refrigerate overnight. Rinse turkey breast, pat dry, and place in a large resealable plastic bag with 1/2 to 1 cup marinade. Marinate in refrigerator for 2 hours or overnight. Over a medium-low fire in a water smoker or covered grill (add a handful of water-soaked apple-wood chips to the coals), smoke turkey for 8 to 10 hours, basting every hour with additional marinade. Add more chips about every 2 hours, and maintain a medium-low fire with more briquettes as needed. Turkey is done when internal temperature reaches 170 degrees on a meat thermometer.

SERVES 6–8

Kansas Citians keep their grills stoked and ready 12 months a year, so a wood-smoked Christmas turkey is a familiar dish in our town. Carolyn Wells, an award-winning leader in local and national barbecue circles, has shared this favorite recipe of hers, which she once prepared for a group of food writers at Tavern on the Green. It pairs well with an apple-based salsa or relish.

Pheasant Madeira

4 pheasant breasts, boned and skinned
1 cup all-purpose flour, seasoned with salt and pepper
1 egg
3/4 cup buttermilk
1/4 cup (1/2 stick) butter
1/2 cup Madeira wine
1 cup sliced shiitake mushrooms
1/4 cup drained capers
3 cups chicken stock
1 cup heavy cream

Dredge pheasant breasts in flour. Combine egg and buttermilk, and dip breasts into mixture. Dredge again in flour. Melt butter and sauté breasts over medium heat, cooking for 4 to 5 minutes on each side. Heat wine to boiling and add mushrooms and capers. When wine is reduced by half, add chicken stock, heavy cream, and pheasant breasts. Cover and simmer for 1 hour. Serve breasts topped with sauce.

SERVES 4

Pheasant is usually plentiful here in the fall and winter months, making it a natural entree for Christmastide repasts. The distinctive taste of Madeira cloaks these game birds in a rich "Old World" holiday spirit.

Chicken Alouette

Although poultry figures prominently in most Christmas-season menus, sometimes chicken is overlooked as too ordinary. Not so—even a visiting Scrooge would be impressed by this "gift-wrapped" version from Karen Zecy, which she serves the night the godparents come over to open presents with her family.

1 (17-1/4-ounce) package frozen puff pastry sheets, thawed
1 (4-ounce) package garlic-and-spice Alouette cheese
6 boneless, skinless chicken breast halves
1/2 teaspoon salt
1/8 teaspoon pepper
1 egg beaten with 1 tablespoon water

On a lightly floured surface, unfold pastry sheets and roll out each into a 14-by-12-inch rectangle. Cut 1 sheet into four 7-by-6-inch rectangles. Cut second sheet into two 7-by-6-inch rectangles and one 7-by-12-inch rectangle. Set large rectangle aside, and spread small rectangles with cheese. Sprinkle breasts with salt and pepper, and place in centers of pastry. Lightly moisten pastry edges with water. Fold ends over chicken, then sides, and press to seal. Place bundles seam-side down on a lightly greased baking sheet. Cut remaining pastry rectangle into 12 strips. Twist strips and lay 2 across each bundle, 1 side to side and 1 top to bottom, tucking ends under. Cover and refrigerate for up to 2 hours if desired. Preheat oven to 400 degrees. Brush beaten egg over bundles and bake on lower rack for 25 minutes, or until golden brown.

SERVES 6

Chicken Scampi

Simple chicken can also stand in well for fancier culinary cousins. In this adaptation of a classic seafood dish, cubed breast meat substitutes for the usual shrimp or lobster and swims in a colorful holiday sauce that features chopped red tomatoes and bits of green parsley.

2 pounds chicken breasts
1/2 cup (1 stick) butter
1/4 cup olive oil
1/4 cup chopped green onions
2 cloves garlic, minced
Juice of 1 lemon
1 teaspoon salt
1/2 teaspoon pepper
1/4 cup minced fresh parsley
1 tomato, chopped
Buttered noodles

Skin and debone chicken. Cut into 1/2-inch pieces and rinse thoroughly. Heat butter and olive oil, and sauté green onions and garlic. Add lemon juice, chicken pieces, salt, pepper, and parsley. Continue cooking, stirring constantly, for 5 to 8 minutes, or until chicken is done. Add tomatoes and heat through. Serve over noodles.

SERVES 4–6

Pollo Alla Royale Daniele

2 pounds skinless chicken parts (legs, breasts, thighs)
All-purpose flour
1/2 cup olive oil
1 cup dry white wine
1/4 teaspoon dried tarragon
4 sprigs fresh rosemary
4 cloves garlic, minced
6–8 skinned and chopped Roma tomatoes
Salt to taste
Pinch of cayenne pepper
1 cup reduced-fat chicken broth
2 large potatoes, cut into 1/2-inch cubes
8 sliced fresh mushrooms

Preheat oven to 400 degrees. Dust each chicken piece with flour and place in a large baking dish. Add olive oil, wine, tarragon, rosemary, garlic, and tomatoes. Season with salt and cayenne pepper. Roast for 15 minutes, then add broth, potatoes, and mushrooms. Roast for 45 minutes more, then serve at once.

SERVES 4–6

J.J. Mirabile, scion of the restaurant family that serves so superbly at the corner of 75th and Wornall, shared this redolent recipe for chicken. A tasty example of cucina leggera, this low-fat dish bobs like a delicious buoy in the sea of holiday calories.

Salmon with Red Pepper Butter Sauce

8 salmon steaks, 1-inch thick
Vegetable oil

SAUCE:
1/4 cup plus 2 tablespoons butter
2 tablespoons olive oil
3 shallots, chopped
1 teaspoon honey
1/2 cup chopped roasted, peeled, and seeded red bell pepper
Dash of salt
Freshly ground pepper to taste

Melt butter over low heat, add oil, and sauté shallots until softened but not brown. Remove from heat, stir in honey until dissolved, and cool slightly. Puree peppers in a blender or food processor, and while machine is running on low, slowly pour in butter mixture and whirl until smooth. Transfer to a bowl and season to taste. (Note: For a creamier version, heat sauce slightly and whisk in 1/2 cup heavy cream.) Brush salmon steaks with oil and grill or broil until fish turns opaque and flakes (about 10 minutes), turning once while cooking. Serve with sauce.

SERVES 8

Another satisfying alternative to weighty traditional Christmas fare is fish—grilled, baked, or broiled. The wonderful red pepper butter sauce for this salmon came from Ken Hornung, who fixed it the first time he met his wife's relatives at a family reunion. They set up chairs and benches around the grill to watch—even holiday pressures can't come close to that!

Standing Rib Roast of Beef

Straight out of the storybooks, a beautiful standing rib roast of beef makes quite a centerpiece to a Yuletide feast. Carving at the table presents the perfect opportunity for a round of appreciative oohs and ahhs, the perfect "Christmas carol" to a cook's ears.

1 (10-pound) standing rib roast of beef (4 ribs)
2 teaspoons salt
1 teaspoon freshly ground pepper
1 teaspoon dried thyme

Have butcher trim roast, remove spinal cord, shoulder bone, and chine, and then tie chine back on to preserve contour and protect eye of roast during cooking. Score fat. Combine seasonings well and rub onto entire surface of meat. Place roast on a rack (fat-side up) in a large shallow roasting pan and let stand at room temperature for 1 hour. Preheat oven to 500 degrees. Roast meat for 10 minutes, then reduce temperature to 350 degrees and continue cooking for 18 to 20 minutes per pound for medium-rare (a meat thermometer inserted in thickest part, not touching bone or fat, will register 140 degrees for rare, 170 degrees for well done). Do not baste during roasting. After removing from oven, place roast on its side on a warmed serving platter and cover with a foil tent to hold heat. Carve at table when ready to serve.

SERVES 10–12

Garlic-Stuffed Sirloin

Another cut of beef to consider for the holiday table is a thick, lean sirloin steak. After stuffing goodies into this one's pouch, you'll feel like the jolly old elf himself.

1 (3-pound) boneless beef top sirloin steak, 2 inches thick
1/4 cup garlic cloves, finely chopped
1 tablespoon olive oil
1/2 cup thinly sliced green onions
1/4 teaspoon salt
1/4 teaspoon freshly ground pepper

Sauté garlic in oil over low heat until tender (about 5 minutes). Add onions, increase heat to medium-low, and continue cooking until onions become tender-crisp (about 5 minutes). Stir in salt and pepper, remove from heat, and set aside to cool thoroughly. Make a horizontal cut through center of one side of steak, forming a pocket parallel to surface. (Pocket edges should end about 1 inch from each side, cutting to, but not through, opposite side.) Spoon cooled onion-garlic mixture evenly into pocket, then secure opening with wooden toothpicks. Place steak on prepared grill over medium-low coals. Cover and grill for 25 to 30 minutes, turning once (rare will register 140 degrees on a meat thermometer, medium will register 160 degrees). Remove toothpicks and cut steak into 1/2-inch slices.

SERVES 8

Pepper Veal

1/2 large onion, sliced
8 mushrooms, sliced
2 tablespoons vegetable oil
2 tablespoons all-purpose flour
1 pound veal scallops, pounded thin
1-1/2 cups beef broth
1/4–1/3 cup barbecue sauce
1 (10-ounce) canned roasted red peppers
4 slices Swiss cheese

Sauté onion and mushrooms in 1 tablespoon oil until tender. Set aside and sprinkle with flour, stirring flour through vegetables. Sauté meat slices in remaining 1 tablespoon oil until cooked through (about 2 to 3 minutes). Pour in beef broth, and then add onion-mushroom mixture, barbecue sauce, and peppers. Stir and heat until sauce thickens. Place cheese slices over meat, and spoon some sauce on top of cheese. Heat until cheese melts, then serve.

SERVES 3–4

Every Christmas Eve the Moffat household hosts a dinner for both sides of the family and presents a dinner from a specific national cuisine. This veal entree is one of the courses that Kay developed while trying to duplicate a dish from her favorite German restaurant in Heidelberg. She notes that you can substitute pork tenderloin and also get delicious results.

Pork Tenderloin with Plum Sauce

1 (1-1/2-pound) pork tenderloin
1/4 cup vegetable oil
1/4 cup bourbon or sherry
1/4 cup soy sauce
1/4 cup firmly packed brown sugar
3 cloves garlic, minced

SAUCE:
1 cup plum jelly
1/2 cup chutney
1 teaspoon white vinegar
1 teaspoon sugar

In a glass baking dish, combine oil, bourbon, soy sauce, brown sugar, and garlic, and blend well. Add pork tenderloin, turning several times to coat. Cover and marinade in refrigerator for 2 to 3 hours. Combine sauce ingredients in a blender or food processor and whirl until smooth. Refrigerate sauce, covered, until ready to use. Preheat oven to 400 degrees. Remove pork from marinade and roast for 30 to 35 minutes, or until no longer pink at thickest part (turn once or twice during cooking). Let meat stand for 5 minutes, then slice diagonally. Serve with plum sauce on the side, either warmed or at room temperature.

SERVES 4–6

Another wonderful rendering of pork tenderloin awaits your guests in this version paired with Peggi Kilroy's delectable plum sauce. Peggi also shared the marinade here, which comes together quickly in a blender or food processor.

Gift-Wrapped Ham

Ham is the entree of choice for many families at Christmas, a big one baked with pineapple rings, whole cloves, and often a sugary sweet glaze. For those whose tastes lean toward the smaller, savory side, here's a pastry-wrapped alternative that's in and out of the oven in about an hour.

1 (3-pound) boneless precooked ham
1 (9-inch) pie crust, unbaked
1 egg, beaten
1 tablespoon dried parsley flakes
1-1/2 teaspoons dry mustard
2 teaspoons rubbed sage

Preheat oven to 350 degrees. Lay pie crust out flat and cut out corners to form a cross. Brush with some beaten egg and sprinkle evenly with parsley flakes, dry mustard, and sage. Set ham in center and fold up sides to cover. Pinch edges of pastry to seal and brush surface with remaining beaten egg. Bake for 50 to 60 minutes.

SERVES 6–8

Pasta with Roasted Vegetables

Pasta is also a satisfying change for taste buds suffering from "turkey fatigue." This recipe comes from Maraline Hayob, whose family likes to round out the vegetarian entree with a Caesar salad and a chewy loaf of Italian bread.

1 small eggplant, cut into 1/2-inch pieces
2 yellow squash, cut into 1/2-inch slices
1 red onion, cut into 1/2-inch pieces
1 red bell pepper, cut into 1/2-inch pieces
1 yellow bell pepper, cut into 1/2-inch pieces
1 green bell pepper, cut into 1/2-inch pieces
4 cloves garlic, peeled and halved
1/4–1/3 cup olive oil
1/4 cup finely chopped parsley
2 teaspoons chopped fresh thyme
1/2 teaspoon red pepper flakes (optional)
Salt and pepper to taste
12 ounces radiatori or bowtie pasta
2 tablespoons freshly grated Parmesan cheese

Preheat oven to 400 degrees. Put vegetables and garlic in a large resealable plastic bag, then add olive oil and toss. Spread on roasting pan and bake, turning often, until brown and tender (about 40 minutes). Season with half of parsley, thyme, and red pepper flakes, plus salt and pepper to taste. Cook and drain pasta, reserving 1/2 cup of cooking liquid. Stir remaining red pepper flakes into reserved liquid and let stand for 10 to 30 minutes, then stir. In a serving bowl, toss pasta with half the vegetables, seasoned cooking liquid, and cheese. Spoon on remaining vegetables and top with remaining parsley and thyme. Serve with additional cheese.

SERVES 4–6

Mushroom-Prosciutto Lasagna

1 ounce dried porcini mushrooms
2 pounds fresh mushrooms, chopped coarsely
1/4 cup olive oil
1/4 cup (1/2 stick) plus 2 tablespoons butter
1 medium onion, chopped finely
1 (14-1/2-ounce) can Italian plum tomatoes, drained and
    coarsely chopped
1/4 cup chopped Italian parsley
Salt and freshly ground pepper to taste
16 ounces lasagna noodles, cooked
4 ounces Parmesan cheese, grated
6 ounces prosciutto ham, sliced thinly

SAUCE:
1/2 cup (1 stick) butter
1/3 cup all-purpose flour
4 cups milk
1 teaspoon ground nutmeg
Salt to taste

Preheat oven to 425 degrees and thoroughly grease a 9-by-12-inch baking dish. Place porcini mushrooms in warm water to soak for 30 minutes. Over medium-high heat, sauté fresh mushrooms in oil and 1/4 cup butter until liquid has been released and evaporates. Set aside. Remove porcini mushrooms from water (reserve liquid), then rinse and chop coarsely. Add porcini, onion, tomatoes, and parsley to sautéed mushrooms, then strain reserved mushroom liquid into skillet through a sieve lined with paper towels. Partially cover pan and cook until liquid evaporates. Season with salt and pepper, and set aside.

To make sauce, melt butter, then gradually add flour and stir over low heat for 3 to 5 minutes. Slowly stir in milk, then simmer over medium heat until thickened and smooth (about 8 to 10 minutes). Season with nutmeg and salt, and set aside.

Line bottom of prepared baking dish with one-fourth of lasagna noodles (overlapping slightly). Spread one-third of mushroom mixture over noodles, then top with one-fourth of sauce, one-fourth of Parmesan cheese, and one-third of prosciutto. Repeat sequence twice more (noodles, mushrooms, sauce, Parmesan, and prosciutto). Cover with remaining noodles, then remaining sauce and Parmesan. Dot top with remaining 2 tablespoons butter, cut into small pieces. Bake for 20 to 25 minutes, or until Parmesan is melted and golden brown on top. Let stand for 10 minutes before serving.

SERVES 6–8

For a buffet table or sit-down affair, lasagna never lacks company appeal. This one, prepared with a luscious béchamel sauce and woodsy wild porcini mushrooms, is especially nice for New Year's Eve entertaining. When selecting the dried porcini, choose those that are tan to pale brown, and pass on any that show signs of crumbling.

Pasta Paella

Ellen and Brian Young love to experiment with pasta when they entertain. A small jar of blackening spice teamed up with a pound of imported pasta and this delicious recipe inscribed on a gift card would also create a tasty holiday remembrance for neighborhood friends or co-workers.

1/4 cup (1/2 stick) butter or margarine
4 cloves garlic, crushed
1/2 cup chopped green onions
2 boneless, skinless chicken breast halves, diced
2 Italian sausages, cut into 1-inch slices and browned
8–12 large shrimp, peeled, deveined, and cooked
16 ounces linguine, cooked
2 cups chicken stock
1 cup heavy cream
1/4 cup blackening spice (recipe follows)

BLACKENING SPICE:
1-1/2 teaspoons dried thyme
1 tablespoon dried oregano
1 tablespoon dried basil
1/2 cup paprika
2 tablespoons granulated garlic
2 tablespoons onion powder
3-1/2 tablespoons salt
1-1/2 tablespoons black pepper
1-1/2 tablespoons white pepper
1 tablespoon cayenne pepper

Combine blackening spice ingredients and store in a tightly covered jar. Melt butter or margarine and sauté garlic and green onions for 1 minute. Add chicken and cook until chicken begins to turn white. Add cooked sausage, shrimp, pasta, and chicken stock, and simmer for 2 minutes. Add cream and heat to reduce for 1 minute. When ingredients have heated through, stir 1/4 cup blackening spice into mixture and serve.

SERVES 4–6

Pasta with Vodka Sauce and Sun-Dried Tomatoes

Another great way to remember the special people on your list requires no ribbon or giftwrap, and is always the right size and color—invite them over on a quiet weeknight for a glass of wine and a plate of this savvy pasta from Trattoria Marco Polo.

16 ounces penne or other tubular pasta
5 tablespoons unsalted butter
1/2 cup julienned sun-dried tomatoes
2/3 cup vodka (preferably Polish or Russian)
1/4 teaspoon dried red pepper flakes
1 (16-ounce) can Roma tomatoes, drained, seeded, and pureed
3/4 cup heavy cream
1/2 teaspoon salt
3/4 cup freshly grated Parmesan cheese

In a large pot of boiling salted water, cook pasta until al dente (about 8 to 10 minutes). While pasta cooks, melt butter in a large, noncorrodible skillet over medium heat. Add sun-dried tomatoes and sauté for 3 to 5 minutes. Stir in vodka and pepper flakes, and simmer for 2 minutes. Add pureed tomatoes and cream, simmering for 5 minutes more. Season with salt. When pasta is cooked, drain well and add to skillet with hot sauce. Reduce heat to low, add cheese, and mix thoroughly. Pour into a heated bowl and serve at once.

SERVES 4

Curried Pumpkin-Leek Soup

3 tablespoons butter
1 bunch leeks, sliced and soaked in water for 30 minutes, then rinsed
    and drained
1 (16-ounce) can pumpkin
1 (16-ounce) can Italian tomatoes
4 cups chicken or vegetable stock
1 bay leaf
1 teaspoon sugar
1/2 teaspoon cayenne pepper
1/2 teaspoon white pepper
1/2 teaspoon ground turmeric
1/2 teaspoon ground cinnamon
1/2 teaspoon ground coriander
1/2 teaspoon ground ginger
4 cups half-and-half or milk
Grated nutmeg, sour cream, and chopped green onions

Melt butter and sauté leeks until soft. Add pumpkin, tomatoes, stock, bay leaf, and sugar. Combine peppers, turmeric, cinnamon, coriander, and ginger in a small dry sauté pan and toast gently over low heat, jiggling the pan. When aromas become strong, remove from heat, add to soup, and simmer for about 15 minutes. Remove from heat and whirl in batches in a food processor until blended. When ready to serve, return to heat and stir in half-and-half (do not boil). Top portions with nutmeg, a dollop of sour cream, and green onions.

SERVES 8

Kansas City food guru Lou Jane Temple supplied this smooth, fragrant concoction, which she refers to as her "holiday soup." For anyone who has only encountered pumpkin in a crust under a dollop of whipped cream, this soup will provide a pleasant, flavorful reeducation.

Smooth Butternut Squash Soup

Winter squashes such as butternut and acorn are versatile menu items that can be baked, steamed, or simmered with equal success. They also lend themselves well to either sweet or savory seasonings. Linda Buchner has turned one of these seasonal staples into a delicious soup, sure to strike just the right note after days of holiday indulgence.

4-1/2 pounds butternut squash, halved lengthwise
1/4 cup (1/2 stick) butter
4–5 large leeks, sliced thinly (white and tender green parts)
8 sprigs fresh thyme or 1-1/2 teaspoons dried leaves
5 cups chicken or vegetable stock
Salt and pepper taste
Dried red pepper flakes to taste
1/2 cup sour cream
2–3 tablespoons chopped fresh chives
8 slices bacon, fried crisp and crumbled

Preheat oven to 350 degrees. Scrape out seeds from squash and place halves cut-side down on a baking sheet. Bake until tender (about 40 minutes, depending on size). Cool slightly, then scrape out pulp and reserve. While squash is baking, melt butter over low heat. Add leeks and thyme, and cook, stirring occasionally, until soft and slightly browned (about 50 minutes). Remove thyme sprigs, stir in stock and squash pulp, and simmer over medium-low heat for about 20 minutes. Transfer to a blender or food processor and puree in batches until smooth. Pour soup back into pan and season with salt, pepper, and pepper flakes. To serve, ladle into bowls and garnish each with a dollop of sour cream, a sprinkling of chives, and a few crumbled pieces of bacon.

SERVES 8

Celebration Soup

Susan and Judy Jackson also have a way with soup, and here they share one that friends look forward to at their annual holiday luncheon. The recipe originated with Susan and Judy's mother-in-law, and it's a much-enjoyed accompaniment to the handmade gifts they also prepare for the occasion.

3 tablespoons butter
3 carrots, grated
3 stalks celery, chopped
3 green onions, chopped (white and green parts)
2 (14-1/2-ounce) cans chicken broth
2 (10-3/4-ounce) cans cream of potato soup
1 cup milk
1 cup sour cream
1 pound Old English cheese loaf

Melt butter and sauté carrots, celery, and onions. Add chicken broth and simmer for 30 minutes. Add potato soup, milk, sour cream, and cheese. Heat until cheese melts.

SERVES 12

Oyster Stew

4 cups milk
1 cup heavy cream
1/2 cup (1 stick) butter
3 pints fresh oysters with 4 cups liquid
2 teaspoons salt
Dash of pepper
Dash of Worcestershire sauce (optional)
Oyster crackers

Combine milk and cream, and heat to scalding. In another pan, melt butter and add oysters with liquid. Cook gently, just until oyster edges curl. Add to scalded milk–cream mixture and season with salt, pepper, and Worcestershire sauce. Serve immediately with oyster crackers.

SERVES 8

Pints of fresh oysters are readily available during the holidays, for stuffings as well as treats such as this creamy stew. Daria Blankenship traces the recipe back at least 50 years in her family, to a Christmas Eve tradition started by her grandmother. Plenty of oyster crackers are a must.

Mock Turtle Soup

2 pounds beef knuckles or soup bone
Salt to taste
6 whole cloves
1/2 teaspoon peppercorns
6 allspice berries
2 sprigs fresh thyme
1/2 cup sliced onion
1/3 cup diced carrot
1/4 cup (1/2 stick) butter
1/2 cup all-purpose flour
2 cups brown stock
1 cup stewed, strained tomatoes
Juice of 1/2 lemon
Madeira wine
Additional salt and pepper to taste

Bring 3 quarts salted water to a boil. Add beef knuckles or soup bone, salt, cloves, peppercorns, allspice berries, thyme, onion, and carrot. Simmer until meat is tender (about 4 hours). Remove soup bone(s) and continue to boil stock until it is reduced to 1 quart. Dice meat from bone(s) and set aside. Strain stock and cool. Melt and brown butter, add flour, and stir until well browned. Slowly pour in brown stock, stirring and mixing well. Add cooled 1 quart stock, diced meat, tomatoes, and lemon juice. Simmer for 5 minutes, then add wine and season to taste with salt and pepper.

SERVES 8–10

Kay Moffat of the Wornall House supplied this tasty variation on old-fashioned mock turtle soup. This version eschews the traditional calf's head, relying instead on less exotic soup bones for flavoring. If making ahead to freeze, omit the wine, which should be added just before serving. Smaller portions of this spice-laced soup also make an appealing appetizer.

Spinach–Italian Sausage Soup

When it's cold outside and you've been shopping all day, Premila Borchardt recommends this hearty spinach soup of her mom's, teamed up with a salad and some French bread or hard rolls.

6 medium baking potatoes, peeled and diced
6 cups chicken broth
2 cups water
3 tablespoons olive oil
1 pound Italian sausage, cut into 1-inch pieces
2 (10-ounce) packages frozen chopped spinach, thawed and
    squeezed dry
Salt and pepper to taste

Boil potatoes in broth and water until soft (about 15 to 20 minutes). Remove potatoes and reserve cooking liquid. Mash potatoes until just slightly lumpy, then return to cooking liquid. Heat oil and brown sausage pieces. Add sausage, spinach, salt, and pepper to potatoes mixture, and simmer for 45 minutes.

SERVES 4–6

Wild Rice Soup

When Caroline McKnight's in-laws gently complained about having to consume two Christmas dinners in one day, she eased back to soup and sandwiches for a holiday lunch. This one serves well in cups and is just right alongside ham or turkey sandwiches on mini buns.

2/3 cup wild rice, rinsed
1/2 cup diced onion
1/2 cup diced celery
1/2 cup diced carrot
4 strips thick-sliced bacon, diced
3 tablespoons unsalted butter, softened
4 to 4-1/2 cups chicken stock
1 to 1-1/2 cups heavy cream
1 tablespoon all-purpose flour
Salt and freshly ground pepper to taste
Chopped fresh parsley or snipped chives

Sauté rice, onion, celery, carrots, and bacon in 2 tablespoons butter until vegetables are crisp-tender (about 3 minutes). Stir in 4 cups stock. Stirring constantly, bring to a boil, then reduce heat. Simmer, covered, until rice is tender (about 30 minutes—rice deteriorates if simmered too long), stirring occasionally. Stir in 1 cup cream. Mix remaining 1 tablespoon butter with flour to make a paste, and whisk into soup to thicken. Cook for 1 minute more, then add additional stock or cream if thinner soup is desired. Season with salt and pepper, and serve garnished with parsley or snipped chives.

SERVES 6–8

Brandy-Spiked Lentil Soup

2 cups lentils, rinsed and drained
1 onion, chopped
1 (14-1/2-ounce) can tomatoes, chopped
4-1/2 cups beef stock
2 cloves garlic, minced
2–4 tablespoons brandy
Salt and pepper to taste
Cayenne pepper to taste

Combine lentils with onion, tomatoes, stock, and garlic, bring to a boil, and then simmer over medium-low heat for 1-1/2 hours. Puree in a blender or food processor, then return to pan, stir in brandy, and season with salt and peppers.

SERVES 8–10

This "velvety potion" was inspired by the late Laurie Colwin. It's hard to think of a better way to relax and "de-stress" during the holidays than to curl up on the couch with a warm mug of this soothing soup and a broken-in copy of one of Laurie's wonderful books.

Three-Bean Turkey Chili

2 to 2-1/2 pounds ground turkey breast
1 (15-ounce) can dark red kidney beans
1 (15-ounce) can white kidney beans
1 (15-ounce) can pinto beans
1 (15-ounce) can tomato sauce
1 (15-ounce) can diced tomatoes
2 (4-ounce) cans chopped green chilies
1 large onion, chopped
1 large green bell pepper, chopped
1 to 1-1/2 cups corn kernels (optional)
3 cloves garlic, minced
1 tablespoon ground cumin
1 to 1-1/2 tablespoons chili powder (or to taste)
1 bay leaf
Salt and pepper to taste
Reduced-fat chicken broth
Grated low-fat Monterey Jack cheese (optional)

Spray bottom of a Dutch oven with nonstick cooking spray and brown turkey meat. Stir in beans, tomato sauce, vegetables, and seasonings (do not drain any of the canned items), and bring mixture to a boil. Thin with broth as necessary. Reduce heat, cover, and simmer for about 2 hours, stirring occasionally. Adjust seasonings and add broth as desired. Remove bay leaf and refrigerate chili for 3 to 4 hours, then reheat before serving. Sprinkle portions with grated cheese if desired.

SERVES 8–10

Soups often come together much like quilts—a scrap of this, a patch of that. This turkey chili easily accommodates other ingredients, either as additions or as substitutions. If a lonely stalk of celery is left after the open house buffet, here's the place for it.

Garnished Baked Potato Soup

This delicious potato soup is perfect for casual partying because the garnishes are "self-serve." Provide the various suggested toppings (plus any others, such as chopped jalapeños) in pretty bowls around the tureen and let guests create their own palette of flavors.

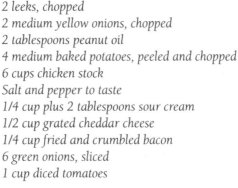

2 leeks, chopped
2 medium yellow onions, chopped
2 tablespoons peanut oil
4 medium baked potatoes, peeled and chopped
6 cups chicken stock
Salt and pepper to taste
1/4 cup plus 2 tablespoons sour cream
1/2 cup grated cheddar cheese
1/4 cup fried and crumbled bacon
6 green onions, sliced
1 cup diced tomatoes

Sauté leeks and onions in peanut oil until translucent. Add potatoes and chicken stock. Simmer for 20 minutes, then season with salt and pepper. Whisk in sour cream and heat through. Garnish individual portions with cheese, bacon, green onions, and tomatoes.

SERVES 6–8

Sunflower Split-Pea Soup

Soup mixes based on dried legumes and seasonings can make appealing gifts for teachers, hair dressers, and other special people. For this one, place the sunny split peas in a pretty glass jar and tuck in a small plastic bag containing the seasonings and bouillon cubes. Attach the recipe and a silk sunflower to add a Heartland flourish.

2 cups dried yellow split peas
1 large onion, diced
1 stalk celery, diced
1 carrot, diced
1 tablespoon vegetable oil
1 tablespoon Italian seasoning
1 tablespoon garlic powder
1 teaspoon onion salt
2 beef bouillon cubes
2 vegetable bouillon cubes
4–6 cups water

Rinse and sort peas. Cover with water and simmer for 3 to 5 minutes. Remove from heat, cover pan, and set aside for 1 hour. Drain and set aside. Sauté onion, celery, and carrot in oil for 5 minutes, then add peas, seasonings, bouillon cubes, and water. Simmer over medium-low heat for 2 to 3 hours, or until done. Adjust seasonings and serve.

SERVES 8–10

Cheese and Spinach Quiche

1 (9-inch) deep-dish pie crust, baked
2–3 tablespoons finely chopped onions
1/4 cup (1/2 stick) butter
2 tablespoons all-purpose flour
3 eggs, beaten
1 (16-ounce) carton cream-style small curd cottage cheese
6 ounces Old English cheese, grated
1 (10-ounce) package frozen chopped spinach, thawed and
     squeezed dry
1 pound bacon, chopped and baked until crisp

Preheat oven to 350 degrees. Sauté onions in butter until soft. Combine onions and butter with flour, eggs, cottage cheese, Old English cheese, and spinach, then pour mixture into prepared pie crust. Sprinkle bacon evenly over top. Bake for 50 to 60 minutes, then let stand for 10 minutes before serving.

SERVES 6–8

Quiche is a simple, often elegant one-dish solution to the question of what to serve for light holiday dinners or brunches. This one was a perennial favorite from the kitchen of the old Junior League headquarters on the Plaza, and Jo Riley shares it here with many fond memories.

Sausage-Apple Ring

2 pounds bulk sausage
1-1/2 cups crushed cracker crumbs
2 eggs, slightly beaten
1/2 cup milk
1/4 cup onion, minced
1 cup finely chopped apple
Scrambled eggs

Preheat oven to 350 degrees. Thoroughly combine sausage, cracker crumbs, eggs, milk, onion, and apple. Press lightly into a greased ring mold, then turn out into a shallow baking pan or sheet cake pan. Bake for 1 hour. (Note: May be baked partially for 30 minutes, then drain fat, refrigerate, and finish baking when ready to serve.) Drain well before placing on a serving platter. Fill center with scrambled eggs and serve.

SERVES 10–12

Also with a Junior League past (this one from Huntsville, Alabama), this ring offers a no-fail meat entree for brunches and scrambled egg suppers. Caroline McKnight found this recipe years ago in a JL Huntsville cookbook and has adopted it as a constant in her holiday repertoire.

Christmas Morning Casserole

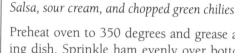

Breakfast casseroles are just right for Christmas morning, but who wants to spend time in the kitchen when there are presents to open? This one (adapted from Nancy McKay's) assembles quickly and easily, then it's into the oven and ready to eat when the last piece of wrapping paper flutters to the floor.

1-1/2 cups chopped ham
1 cup shredded Monterey Jack cheese
1/2 cup shredded cheddar cheese
12 eggs
1-1/2 cups milk
Salsa, sour cream, and chopped green chilies

Preheat oven to 350 degrees and grease a 9-by-12-inch glass baking dish. Sprinkle ham evenly over bottom, followed by cheeses. With the back of a spoon, slightly hollow 12 places for eggs (away from edge of glass). Break eggs into indentations, and lightly break yolks with a fork. Pour milk on top and bake for 35 to 45 minutes (depending on preference for hard- or soft-cooked eggs). Serve with salsa, sour cream, and green chilies on the side.

SERVES 8–10

Make-Ahead Breakfast Eggs

Even better sometimes is a casserole that holds overnight. After tiptoeing down the stairs on Christmas morning to turn on the tree for the children, slide this dish of Judi Walker's into the oven, and breakfast will be ready when the stomach growls get louder than the carols playing in the background.

6–8 bread slices, crusts removed and one side buttered
1/2 cup sliced fresh mushrooms
3/4 cup chopped onion
1/2 cup chopped green bell pepper
2–3 tablespoons butter or margarine
1 cup shredded cheddar cheese
6 eggs, well beaten
2-1/2 cups milk
1 pound mild bulk sausage, fried, drained, and crumbled
1 teaspoon salt
1/2 teaspoon pepper
1 teaspoon dry mustard
1/2 teaspoon garlic salt

Arrange bread slices in the bottom of a 9-by-12-inch baking dish, buttered side up. Sauté mushrooms, onions, and green pepper in butter until soft, then combine with remaining ingredients and pour over bread. Cover with foil and refrigerate overnight. Preheat oven to 350 degrees. Uncover baking dish and bake for 1 hour or until set.

SERVES 10–12

Side Dishes

*Fruits, Vegetables,
Casseroles, & Stuffings*

Layered Apples and Onions

5 onions, sliced thinly
5 apples, peeled, cored, and sliced thinly
5 or more strips bacon, fried and crumbled (reserve drippings)
About 1/2 cup beef consommé or bouillon
1/4–1/2 cup bread crumbs

Preheat oven to 350 degrees. In a greased casserole, arrange alternating layers of onions, apples, and bacon bits. Pour consommé over top. Brown bread crumbs in some reserved bacon drippings and use as a topping. Bake covered for about 30 minutes, then uncover and bake for 10 to 15 minutes more.

SERVES 6–8

This homey combination came from Katharine Shaw, who often made it her contribution at holiday potlucks. When she and her husband hosted these communal feasts, the ambience of their beautiful old Lexington home swept friends merrily into the spirit of Christmas past.

Spiced Peaches

1 (29-ounce) can peach halves
1/2 cup firmly packed brown sugar
1/2 cup white wine vinegar
2 cinnamon sticks
1 teaspoon whole cloves
1 teaspoon ground allspice

Drain peaches and reserve syrup. Combine syrup, brown sugar, vinegar, cinnamon, cloves, and allspice, and bring to a boil. Add peaches and simmer for 5 minutes. Refrigerate overnight in syrup. (Note: Use less vinegar for less "bite.")

SERVES 10–12

Spiced fruit is an oldtime holiday tradition in many parts of the country. This version from Karen Zecy easily serves as a gift when put up in jars tied with ribbon.

Cold Green Beans with Sour Cream

Caroline McKnight shared these beans, a tradition at her Grandmother Hampton's spread when the family gathered on Christmas Day. The usual menu consisted of turkey and dressing, cold green beans, turnip greens, and Texas Ruby Red grapefruit sections with avocado slices and poppy seed dressing.

1 tablespoon vegetable oil
2 tablespoons white vinegar
Salt and pepper to taste
2 (16-ounce) cans whole Blue Lake green beans, rinsed and drained,
    or 32 ounces frozen beans, blanched for 2 minutes
1 cup sour cream
1/2 cup mayonnaise
1/4 teaspoon dry mustard
1/2 tablespoon prepared horseradish (or more to taste)
1/2 teaspoon onion juice or 1/4 cup finely minced onion
2 tablespoons chopped fresh chives

Combine oil, vinegar, salt, and pepper, and pour over beans. Cover and marinate in refrigerator for 2 to 3 hours or overnight. Combine sour cream, mayonnaise, mustard, horseradish, and onion. Stir into beans and refrigerate until ready to serve. Sprinkle chopped chives on top before serving.

SERVES 6–8

Green Beans and Country Ham

Back in Kentucky at the holidays, the Doyle family always brings out a country ham, which steadily disappears after Christmas dinner into breakfast eggs and lunchtime sandwiches (any excuse to nibble will do). These beans can be made with bacon in lieu of ham, and adding corn to the mix makes a delicious succotash.

1-1/2 to 2 cups country ham pieces
1 onion, chopped finely
2–3 cloves garlic, minced
Dash of Worcestershire sauce
3 (15-ounce) cans cut green and shelly beans
Freshly ground pepper to taste

Heat country ham pieces until fat is released, then add onion, garlic, and Worcestershire sauce. sauté until onion becomes translucent, then stir in beans (including liquid) and season with pepper to taste. Simmer over low heat for 2 to 3 hours, stirring occasionally, until beans are well seasoned.

SERVES 10–12

Brussels Sprouts with Chestnuts

2 cups small fresh Brussels sprouts, trimmed, rinsed, and drained
1-1/2 cups canned chestnuts, drained
1/2 cup (1 stick) butter, melted
1 teaspoon ground mace
1/2 teaspoon salt
2 tablespoons heavy cream

Bring Brussels sprouts to a boil in just enough water to cover, then cover pan and simmer over medium heat until just tender (about 20 minutes). Drain, return to pan, and set aside. Cook chestnuts in boiling water for 15 minutes. Drain and add to Brussels sprouts, followed by butter, mace, salt, and cream. Stir to combine, then simmer for 5 minutes. Serve hot.

SERVES 4–6

There's no reason to consign chestnuts to an open fire at the holidays—they also can be boiled, pureed, preserved, or candied. Try them in desserts or in savory side dishes such as turkey stuffing or these tasty sprouts.

Baked Celery Casserole

4 cups (2-inch) celery pieces
1/2 cups slivered almonds
1–2 tablespoons butter
1 (4-ounce) can water chestnuts, drained
1 (10-3/4-ounce) can cream of chicken soup

Preheat oven to 325 degrees. Steam or boil celery until tender, then drain and set aside. Sauté almonds in butter until golden, then combine with celery, water chestnuts, and soup. Transfer to a 1-quart casserole and bake for 1-1/2 hours.

SERVES 6–8

Celery is another ingredient that's underappreciated—always a bridesmaid, never a bride. Jill Adler's mother, Lynda Feuerborn, however, serves this crunchy side dish throughout the holidays, and it's quite a family favorite.

Spinach Soufflé

There's always a spot reserved for this simple soufflé at the Adlers' holiday meal. Part of the tradition also requires a side of creamed spinach for Dick, who likes that better than soufflé. Karen cooks 2 packages of frozen spinach, combines it with a roux of 1/4 cup butter and 1/4 cup flour, stirs in 1/2 cup milk, and then warms all until thick.

2 (10-ounce) packages frozen chopped spinach
1-1/2 cups water
1/2 cup (1 stick) butter
1/2 cup all-purpose flour
1 cup half-and-half
2 eggs, beaten
1/2 cup grated Romano cheese
1/2 cup grated Gruyère cheese

Preheat oven to 350 degrees. Cook spinach in water over medium heat until thawed. Add butter, and when melted, sprinkle flour over spinach and blend in. Let simmer for 3 to 4 minutes, then transfer mixture to a bowl. Add half-and-half and eggs, stir to blend, and then add Romano cheese and blend. Pour mixture into a greased 9-by-12-inch casserole. Top with Gruyère cheese and bake for 30 to 35 minutes, or until a knife inserted comes out clean.

SERVES 8–10

Glazed Carrots and Onions

Carrots add a welcome splash of color to the palette of winter foods. This glazed variety is not difficult to prepare, and it offers a delicate balance of sweetness to the savory elements on the menu.

1 pound baby carrots (about 1-1/2 inches long)
1/2 pound pearl onions, peeled and ends trimmed
3 tablespoons butter
1 cup chicken broth
Salt and freshly ground pepper to taste
2 teaspoons sugar

In a heavy saucepan, melt butter, then add carrots and onions, stirring to coat with butter. Add broth and simmer, covered, over low heat until vegetables are tender (about 20 minutes). About halfway through cooking, stir in salt and pepper. When vegetables are tender, if liquid is not reduced, cook over higher heat for 1 or 2 minutes. Add sugar, cover pan, and shake back and forth for 1 minute. Uncover and cook for 1 minute more, until carrots and onions are well glazed (but not brown).

SERVES 6–8

Fresh Corn Pudding

2 cups fresh corn kernels (about 4 medium ears)
1 tablespoon minced red bell pepper
1/4 cup chopped green onions (white and green parts)
1-1/2 tablespoons all-purpose flour
2 teaspoons sugar
1/4 teaspoon salt
1/4 teaspoon cornstarch
Dash of cayenne pepper
2 eggs
1 cup heavy cream

Preheat oven to 350 degrees. Combine corn, bell pepper, green onions, flour, sugar, salt, and cornstarch, stirring well. Stir together eggs and milk, and add to corn mixture. Spoon mixture into a 1-quart greased casserole. Place dish in a larger shallow pan and add water to depth of 1 inch. Bake for 1 hour, or until a knife inserted comes out clean.

SERVES 6–8

Corn Soufflé

1 (16-ounce) can cream-style corn
2/3 stick margarine, melted
1/4 cup all-purpose flour
1 tablespoon sugar
1/2 teaspoon salt
4 eggs, beaten
1 cup milk

Preheat oven to 325 degrees. Blend corn and margarine, and set aside. In a separate bowl, combine flour, sugar, and salt, then stir into corn mixture. Combine eggs and milk, stir into corn mixture, and then pour combination into a 2-quart casserole. Bake for 45 to 60 minutes.

SERVES 6–8

In the Heartland and elsewhere, corn is a regular comer to the holiday table. Karen Zecy shared both of the recipes appearing here, which present a delicious dilemma in choosing between them. When fresh corn isn't available for the pudding, substitute frozen kernels (thawed first, of course).

Squash Tian

The squashes of winter are hardy souls with thick skins and richly colored flesh. Although many traditional recipes adorn them with sweets and spices, this cheese and garlic treatment is awfully tasty.

2 large butternut squash, peeled, seeded, and cut into 1-inch chunks
1 cup all-purpose flour
1/3 cup freshly grated Parmesan cheese
1 large clove garlic, minced
Freshly ground pepper to taste
1/3 cup olive oil

Preheat oven to 400 degrees. Toss chunks of squash in flour and place in a lightly greased baking dish. Sprinkle with cheese, garlic, and pepper, then drizzle with oil. Bake for 30 to 40 minutes.

SERVES 6–8

Baked Acorn Squash

The cavity in a baked acorn squash half just begs to hold something delicious. Experiment with applesauce or a fruit butter instead, of the usual brown sugar, or swing to the savory side and create an herbed spinach filling.

4 acorn squash, halved, seeds and fibers removed
Salt and pepper to taste
1/2 cup brown sugar
1/4 cup (1/2 stick) butter
1/2 cup rum
Freshly grated nutmeg

Preheat oven to 325 degrees. Place squash halves cut-side down on a rimmed baking sheet and bake for 25 minutes. Remove from oven, turn halves over, and sprinkle cut side with salt and pepper. Into each cavity spoon 1 tablespoon brown sugar, 1/2 tablespoon butter, 1 tablespoon rum, and a grating of nutmeg. Return to oven and bake for 15 to 20 minutes more, or until flesh is tender and easily pierced.

SERVES 8

Mushrooms in Red Wine

2 cloves garlic, sliced
1/2 cup (1 stick) butter
2 pounds fresh mushrooms, sliced
1 tablespoon soy sauce
1/4 cup Burgundy wine
Freshly ground pepper

Sauté garlic in butter until soft. Add mushrooms, stirring for 7 to 10 minutes until coated. Add soy sauce and continue to sauté. When mushrooms begin to cook, add wine and season with pepper. Continue to cook until mushrooms are done and most of wine has cooked off.

SERVES 8

Even though living in Hawaii now, Linda Yeates keeps her Kansas City traditions going strong at the holidays. These wine-laced mushrooms are wonderful alongside seared sirloin or other beef entrees.

Roasted Fennel Potatoes

3 pounds potatoes, peeled and cut into 1-1/2-inch chunks
1/4 cup olive oil
1/4 cup (1/2 stick) butter
2 tablespoons fennel seeds
Salt and pepper to taste

Preheat oven to 250 degrees. Boil potatoes for 1 minute, then drain and set aside. Heat a roasting pan containing olive oil and butter, then add drained potatoes and stir to coat. Bake for 30 minutes. Add fennel seeds, salt, and pepper, and increase oven heat to 400 degrees. Continue baking, stirring from time to time, until potatoes turn crisp and golden (about 30 to 60 minutes).

SERVES 8–10

The old standby roasted potatoes just need a little nudge to become something special for Christmas dinner. The fragrant fennel here adds an interesting depth to this very simple recipe.

Smoked Oyster–Stuffed Potatoes

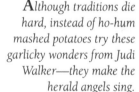

Oysters are not uncommon in stuffing holiday turkeys, but what a delectable surprise to find them hiding in stuffed baked potatoes. As a variation, replace the cheddar cheese, butter, and sour cream with 4 ounces of Boursin or cream cheese.

4 medium baking potatoes, scrubbed and pierced
1 (6-ounce) can smoked oysters, drained
2/3 cup shredded cheddar cheese
3 tablespoons butter or margarine, melted
1/4 cup light sour cream
2 green onions, chopped finely (white and green parts)
1/2 teaspoon salt
1/4 teaspoon black pepper
Dash of cayenne pepper
Paprika

Bake potatoes at 450 degrees until just tender (about 50 minutes). Cut each potato in half lengthwise and scoop out pulp. Combine pulp with oysters, cheese, butter, sour cream, green onions, salt, pepper, and cayenne, then stuff each potato half with mixture and place in a shallow baking pan. Sprinkle each with paprika. (May be made ahead to this point and frozen; thaw before baking.) Reduce oven temperature to 400 degrees and bake for 15 minutes, or microwave at 100% power for 6 to 8 minutes.

SERVES 6–8

Pommes Dauphine

Although traditions die hard, instead of ho-hum mashed potatoes try these garlicky wonders from Judi Walker—they make the herald angels sing.

1 whole clove garlic plus 1–2 crushed cloves
2-1/4 pounds potatoes, peeled and sliced thinly
Salt and pepper to taste
1-1/2 cups grated Gruyère cheese
1/4 cup (1/2 stick) butter, cut into small pieces
1/2 cup heavy cream

Preheat oven to 350 degrees. Rub the inside of a large baking dish with a whole garlic clove, then grease well. Make layers of sliced potatoes, sprinkling each layer with salt, pepper, cheese, some crushed garlic, and dots of butter. Pour cream down sides of dish and over potatoes. Bake for 30 to 40 minutes.

SERVES 8–10

Escalloped Sweet Potatoes

3 medium sweet potatoes, cooked, peeled, and halved
1 unpeeled orange, sliced thinly
1 unpeeled apple, sliced thinly
1 peach, peeled and sliced (or substitute another apple)
1/2 cup water
2 tablespoons honey
2 tablespoons orange juice
2 tablespoons pineapple juice
2 tablespoons firmly packed brown sugar
1 tablespoon butter

TOPPING:
3 tablespoons bread crumbs
2 tablespoons firmly packed brown sugar
1 tablespoon butter
6 large marshmallows
3 maraschino cherries, halved

Preheat oven to 350 degrees. Arrange potato halves in an 8- or 9-inch square pan and top with fruit slices. Combine water, honey, juices, sugar, and butter, and bring to a boil. Pour mixture over potatoes and fruit. For topping, make a crumbly mixture of crumbs, sugar, and butter, and sprinkle over top of potatoes. Bake for 20 minutes, then remove from oven and put a marshmallow on each potato. Bake for 10 minutes more, or until marshmallows are browned. Garnish with cherry halves.

SERVES 6–8

This recipe harkens from one of the landmarks of comfort food in Kansas City. Steve Stephenson of Stephenson's Apple Tree Inn shared these holiday yams, decked in fruited finery that is impressive on a holiday buffet.

Sweet Potato Puree with Lime and Ginger

6 large sweet potatoes, baked
1-inch piece fresh ginger, peeled and grated
1/2 cup firmly packed brown sugar
Juice of 1 lime

When potatoes are cool, scoop out pulp into a blender or food processor. Add other ingredients and puree. Serve either warm (reheated in a microwave or in the oven using a water bath) or at room temperature.

SERVES 6–8

As a very simple, low-fat alternative, food writer Judith Fertig devised these pureed sweet potatoes. The fresh tastes of lime and ginger create a light interpretation of this favorite holiday staple.

Sweet Potato Pancakes

Bonnie Winston's holiday celebrations center around Hanukkah, and this sweet potato version of the traditional latke crosses over deliciously to the Christmas table. Try these accompanied with the traditional sour cream and applesauce.

1 large sweet potato (about 9 ounces), peeled and grated coarsely
1 small onion (about 3 ounces), grated coarsely
1 large egg
2 tablespoons all-purpose flour
1/8 teaspoon ground cardamom
Salt and pepper to taste
Vegetable oil

Combine grated sweet potato and onion with egg, flour, and seasonings. (Note: As a variation, substitute curry powder, ground cumin, or grated fresh ginger for the cardamom.) Heat 1/4-inch oil until almost smoking, then drop in pancake batter by tablespoonful, flattening with the back of a spoon. Fry over medium-high heat for several minutes on each side, until crisp and golden. Drain on paper towels.

SERVES 4–6

Baked Pasta with Three Cheeses

Claims for the last forkful of "Mom's macaroni" have caused many an altercation at the Doyle house during late night raids for holiday leftovers. Although the shell pasta seems to produce the best results, bowtie noodles lend a festive flair at Christmas.

16 ounces medium shell pasta, cooked and drained
3 cups milk
3 cups finely grated sharp cheddar cheese
2 cups finely grated longhorn Colby cheese
1/4 cup (1/2 stick) plus 2 tablespoons butter
1 tablespoon Worcestershire sauce
1/2 teaspoon garlic powder
1/2 cup crushed cornflakes or bread crumbs
1/4 cup grated Parmesan cheese

Preheat oven to 300 degrees. Grease bottom and sides of a 3-quart casserole. Combine milk, cheddar and Colby cheeses, 1/4 cup butter, Worcestershire sauce, and garlic powder. Simmer over low to medium heat, stirring frequently, until cheeses melt completely (if sauce becomes too thick, thin with a little more milk). Place cooked pasta shells in prepared casserole and pour cheese sauce over all, stirring to blend. Top with crumbs and Parmesan, then dot with pieces of remaining 2 tablespoons butter. Bake uncovered for 1 hour.

SERVES 10–12

Wild Rice with Almonds and Mushrooms

1/2 cup (1 stick) butter
1 cup wild rice
1/2 cup slivered almonds
2 tablespoons finely chopped onion
1/2 pound fresh mushrooms, sliced
1 teaspoon salt
2 tablespoons sherry
3 cups chicken broth

In a heavy skillet, melt butter and then add wild rice, almonds, onion, mushrooms, salt, and sherry. Sauté until rice is well coated, stirring frequently. Transfer mixture to a casserole and stir in chicken broth. Cover and refrigerate (or freeze) for several hours. When ready to bake, return to room temperature, then bake at 325 degrees for about 1 hour, or until rice is cooked.

SERVES 6–8

Another Doyle tradition that Jane has continued in Kansas City is this wonderful sherry-laced wild rice casserole. The dish holds well after baking, even on a hot tray, and is a delicious companion to a variety of meats and poultry.

Wheatberry Waldorf Salad

8 seedless oranges, peeled, sliced, and diced
Seedless green grapes, halved, to taste
6 unpeeled Granny Smith apples, cored and diced
1 bunch celery, chopped
2 cups cooked wheatberries
1 cup lightly toasted pecan halves

DRESSING:
1 cup raspberry vinegar
1/2 cup honey
1 cup olive oil

To prepare dressing, pour vinegar and honey into a food processor. With motor running, slowly add olive oil until mixture emulsifies. Set aside. Combine salad ingredients and toss with dressing. Refrigerate for at least 2 hours before serving.

SERVES 8–10

When Lou Jane Temple decided to update one of her favorite holiday salads, she replaced the creamy dressing with a lighter alternative and substituted healthy wheatberries for most of the nuts. The result is a wonderful New Age Waldorf, which combined with diced turkey is terrific "the day after."

Cranberry Supreme Salad

This pretty salad from Ginny Beall originated at Northern Illinois University's Wassail Feast. The juice that drains from the ground cranberries overnight can be kept and used for fruit punch.

4 cups fresh whole cranberries
2 cups sugar
2 cups seedless red grapes, halved
1/2 cup chopped nuts
1 cup heavy cream, whipped
Lettuce leaves (optional)

Grind cranberries or chop in a food processor. Transfer chopped berries to a large strainer, sprinkle with sugar, and drain overnight. After draining, combine with grapes, nuts, and whipped cream, and serve in mounds or on lettuce leaves.

SERVES 8–10

Holiday Strawberry Mold

Doris Hanks at Best of Kansas City has shared here one of her favorite holiday accompaniments for ham. Enjoying strawberries in the middle of winter makes for a real Christmas treat.

1 (3-ounce) package strawberry gelatin
1 cup boiling water
1 small box frozen strawberries
1 cup heavy cream, whipped
1/2 cup chopped pecans

Dissolve gelatin in boiling water, then add frozen strawberries and stir until mixture begins to thicken. Fold in whipped cream, followed by pecans. Spoon into a mold or serving bowl and refrigerate until set.

SERVES 6–8

Molded Pineapple-Pecan Ring

The nice lime "background" in this holiday mold from Martha Doyle is a smooth partner for the sweet pineapple. The gentle crunch of nuts also adds a pleasant texture. For serving, this slices very well.

2 (3-ounce) packages lime gelatin
2 cups boiling water
1 small can crushed pineapple (juice reserved)
2 teaspoons sugar
1 cup heavy cream, whipped
1 (8-ounce) package cream cheese, softened and creamed with a splash of milk
1/2 cup chopped pecans

Dissolve gelatin in boiling water. Stir in reserved pineapple juice and sugar, then chill until almost set. Stir in whipped cream, cream cheese, pineapple, and pecans, and combine well. Spoon into a large ring mold and refrigerate until set.

SERVES 12–14

Raisin, Nut, and Apple Cider Stuffing

12 cups toasted bread cubes
3/4 cup dried onion flakes
1/4 cup dried parsley flakes
1-1/2 teaspoons poultry seasoning
3 teaspoons celery seed
3 teaspoons salt
1/2 teaspoon pepper
1-1/2 cups raisins
1/2 cup chopped pecans
1/2 cup (1 stick) butter or margarine, melted
1 cup apple cider

Combine bread cubes with seasonings, raisins, and pecans, and mix well. Stir in melted butter and apple cider, and mix well again. Spoon into the cavity of a ready-to-cook goose, then close the opening with skewers and lace up tightly.

STUFFS A 10-POUND GOOSE

Stuffings containing dried fruits are delicious companions for Yuletide poultry. This one works for duck as well as goose— about a third of the recipe is sufficient to fill one of these smaller birds.

Toasted Pecan–Cornbread Stuffing

1 pound mild bulk sausage
1 cup (2 sticks) butter
1 onion, chopped finely
1 cup finely chopped celery
1 cup cooked rice
1 cup toasted pecan pieces
1 cup water chestnuts
1 egg
2 packages Pepperidge Farm cornbread dressing
1 tablespoon rubbed sage
1-1/2 teaspoons dried thyme
1/4 teaspoon ground mace
1/4 teaspoon ground nutmeg
Salt and pepper to taste
Chicken broth or milk

Crumble and brown sausage, drain, and transfer to a large bowl. Add butter to pan, and, when melted, sauté onions and celery. Stir sautéed vegetables into sausage, followed by remaining dry ingredients. Add enough broth to moisten. Stuff turkey with mixture. Spoon remainder into a greased, covered casserole, and bake for 30 minutes at 350 degrees.

STUFFS A LARGE TURKEY AND FILLS A CASSEROLE

Old-fashioned cornbread dressing is the taste many families look forward to at the holidays. This version comes from Leslie Whitaker's kitchen, by way of friend and fan Ginny Beall.

Confetti Rice Dressing

Rice-based dressings can offer a satisfying alternative to those made with bread cubes. To use this one as a turkey stuffing, just double the recipe to fill a 12- to 14-pound bird.

1/4 cup (1/2 stick) butter
3 cloves garlic, minced
1 onion, chopped
1 cup sliced fresh mushrooms
1 cup brown rice
2 cups chicken or vegetable stock
1 tablespoon chopped fresh parsley
1/4 teaspoon dried thyme
Salt and freshly ground pepper to taste
1/2 cup diced red bell pepper
1/2 cup diced green bell pepper
1 large carrot, diced
1/2 cup toasted slivered almonds

Melt butter and sauté garlic, onion, and mushrooms. Add rice and stir until rice turns golden. Pour in stock, followed by seasonings. Cover and bring to a boil, then reduce heat and simmer for 25 to 35 minutes. Add diced peppers and carrot, and simmer for 10 minutes more. Remove from heat and let stand, covered, for 10 minutes. Sprinkle almonds on top.

SERVES 4–6

Stuffing in a Pumpkin

From the Friends of Historic Fort Osage comes this unique stuffing presentation. It was very common during the time of the fort to use the last of the pumpkin harvest in this manner—it sweetens the contents delightfully. This is a favorite at the annual "Christmas 1812."

1 pound mild bulk sausage
1 cup water
4 large celery stalks, diced
1 large onion, chopped
1 pound walnuts, chopped
3/4 teaspoon salt
1/4 teaspoon pepper
3 teaspoons rubbed sage
12 cups cooked brown and/or white rice (cook in chicken broth)
1 large pumpkin

Preheat oven to 325 degrees. Over high heat, crumble and cook sausage until well browned. With slotted spoon, remove sausage, and in remaining drippings plus 1 cup water, cook celery and onion until tender. Remove from heat and add sausage, walnuts, spices, and rice, mixing well. Cut top from pumpkin, creating a hole big enough to get seeds out. After scraping out seeds, spoon in dressing. Replace top, set pumpkin in a large bowl, and add water to bowl. Bake for 2 to 3 hours, or until dressing is warmed thoroughly and pumpkin is browned. Serve out of the pumpkin at the table.

SERVES 15–20

SIDE DISHES

Condiments

Relishes, Chutneys,
Salsas, & Spreads

Cranberry Chutney

1 cup fresh whole cranberries
1 large red apple, cored and diced
1/2 cup raisins
1/2 cup frozen apple juice concentrate, thawed
1 teaspoon ground cinnamon
2 tablespoons grated orange zest
2 tablespoons fresh lemon juice
2 tablespoons grated lemon zest
2 tablespoons finely grated fresh ginger
1/2 teaspoon ground allspice

Combine all ingredients and bring to a boil. Lower heat and simmer for 1 hour, stirring occasionally with a wooden spoon. Store in a covered glass or ceramic container in the refrigerator for up to several days. Serve at room temperature.

MAKES ABOUT 2 CUPS

Winter menus are well-suited to the rich tastes and textures of chutney. This one is a favorite of chef Sarah Garney's. She once made sandwiches of turkey, stuffing, and this chutney on whole wheat bread for her family to take on a holiday driving trip to Colorado. Great road food!

Presto Peach Chutney

1-1/2 cups peach preserves
1/2 teaspoon grated fresh ginger
1/3 cup golden raisins
1/4 cup snipped dried apples
1/2 clove garlic, minced finely
1 tablespoon cider vinegar
1 tablespoon fresh lemon juice
1 teaspoon sea salt
1/4 teaspoon ground cinnamon
1/2 teaspoon white pepper

Combine all ingredients and mix well. Set aside for at least 1 hour before serving. Refrigerate unused portions in a tightly covered container.

MAKES ABOUT 2 CUPS

Unlike most chutneys, this one doesn't require cooking. Offer it at brunch as a condiment for omelets or a spread for muffins. It's also a nice partner for cold chicken.

Apricot-Almond Chutney

Debbie Pope brings out this chutney on Christmas Eve, serving it with crackers and cream cheese and a round of sherry.

1 pound dried apricots
4 cups boiling water
8 cloves garlic
2-inch piece fresh ginger, peeled and chopped
1-1/4 cups red wine vinegar
1-1/2 cups sugar
1/2 teaspoon salt
1/4 teaspoon cayenne pepper
1 cup golden raisins
1/2 cup slivered almonds

Pour boiling water over apricots and soak for 2 to 3 hours. Combine garlic, ginger, and 1/4 cup vinegar in a blender or food processor, and whirl until smooth. Drain apricots and combine with garlic mixture in a heavy pot. Add sugar, salt, and pepper, and simmer over medium heat for 1 hour, stirring frequently. Add raisins and cook for 30 minutes more. Add almonds and cook for 10 minutes more. Pour into canning jars, seal, and process.

MAKES ABOUT 4 CUPS

Hot Tomato Conserve

Conserves work well with cheese and crackers, too, but Debbie also uses this one to accompany roasted pork or chicken. She spoons a pool of the conserve onto each serving plate and then arranges the meat slices on top.

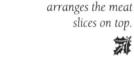

3 pounds ripe tomatoes, seeded and coarsely chopped
3/4 cup firmly packed brown sugar
1 cup cider vinegar
1 large red bell pepper, chopped
1 large onion, coarsely chopped
2 cloves garlic, minced
1/2 cup dark raisins
3 tablespoons minced fresh ginger
2 jalapeño peppers, seeded and chopped
1 teaspoon cumin seeds or 1/2 teaspoon ground cumin
1 teaspoon mustard seeds
1-1/2 teaspoons salt
1/4 cup chopped fresh cilantro

Place all ingredients except cilantro in a large nonaluminum saucepan and simmer over medium heat, stirring until sugar is dissolved. Continue to cook, stirring occasionally, until mixture thickens (about 30 minutes). Stir in cilantro during last few minutes. Pack in sterilized jars, seal, and then freeze or process in a hot water bath.

MAKES 3–4 CUPS

Cilantro Chutney

2 bunches cilantro
1 jalapeño pepper, stem removed
Juice of 2 lemons
1-1/2-inch piece fresh ginger, peeled and grated
1/2 teaspoon salt

Thoroughly rinse cilantro and trim stems 1/2 to 1 inch long. Combine all ingredients in a blender or food processor and whirl until smooth. (Note: Remove seeds from jalapeño for a less spicy chutney.)

MAKES ABOUT 1/2 CUP

Chutneys can range in texture from chunky to smooth, and in taste from mild to spicy hot. Premila Borchardt shared this smooth variety and suggests trying it with meats or as a dip.

Pearl Onion–Cranberry Conserve

1-1/2 cups plus 1 teaspoon firmly packed brown sugar
1 cup water
2 cinnamon sticks
1 tablespoon chopped fresh ginger
1 teaspoon dried grated lemon peel
1 (10-ounce) basket pearl onions
2-1/2 tablespoons unsalted butter
1/8 teaspoon salt
1/4 cup dried currants
3 tablespoons Madeira wine
1 teaspoon red wine vinegar
3 cups fresh whole cranberries
1/2 cup cashews

Combine 1-1/2 cups sugar, water, cinnamon, ginger, and lemon zest, and simmer over medium-high heat until liquids become syrupy (about 10 minutes), stirring occasionally. Set aside. Blanch onions in boiling water for 4 minutes, then drain and rinse under cold water. Peel onions and set aside. Melt butter over medium-high heat, add onions, and sauté until beginning to brown (about 6 minutes). Mix in salt and remaining 1 teaspoon sugar. Add currants and stir for 2 minutes. Add Madeira and vinegar, and stir for 1 minute more. Add sugar mixture, 1-1/2 cups cranberries, and cashews, and cook for 5 minutes, stirring often. Stir in remaining cranberries and simmer until thickened (about 5 minutes), stirring often. Discard cinnamon, cover mixture, and refrigerate for up to 1 week. Let stand for 30 minutes before serving.

MAKES ABOUT 3-1/2 CUPS

The pearl onions and whole cranberries give this conserve an appealing appearance as well as taste. The addition of the rich cashews adds a gentle crunch.

Pretty Peppers

For the holidays, Debbie Pope relies on red and green bell peppers to add "spirit" to this pretty relish, but notes that when available, yellow, orange, and purple peppers are beautiful alternatives. This combination is delightful on warm bruschetta.

6 red bell peppers, finely chopped
6 green bell peppers, finely chopped
1 cayenne or serrano pepper, seeded and finely chopped
7 large onions, cut lengthwise
2 cups cider vinegar
3/4 cup firmly packed brown sugar
1-1/2 teaspoons salt
1 cup fresh thyme sprigs
1/2 cup fresh rosemary sprigs
6 bay leaves

Cover peppers and onions with boiling water and let stand for 10 minutes. Drain, cover with boiling water again, and let stand for 15 minutes more. Add vinegar, sugar, salt, half the thyme and rosemary tied together, and 2 bay leaves, and bring to boil. Cook until just tender (about 15 minutes). Discard thyme-rosemary bundle and bay leaves. Place a fresh thyme or rosemary sprig and 1 bay leaf in each jar, spoon pepper mixture into jars, and then seal and process in a hot water bath.

MAKES 4–5 PINTS

Winter Fruit Relish

Vicki Johnson pairs this dense, delicious relish with turkey, pork, chicken, or ham. One Christmas her son came home from graduate school with the recipe for them to try, and it's been part of their holiday meal traditions every year since.

1 cup dark or golden raisins
2 cups sugar
2 tablespoons white vinegar
1 cup orange juice
2 tablespoons shredded fresh ginger
2 tablespoons slivered orange zest
6 cups (1-1/2 pounds) fresh whole cranberries
1/2 cup diced tart green apples
1 cup slivered almonds, toasted

Cover raisins with boiling water and let stand for 15 minutes. Drain and set aside. In a heavy saucepan, caramelize sugar and vinegar over low heat until golden (takes time—will darken quickly once melted). Add orange juice, bring to a boil, and stir until caramelized sugar dissolves. Add ginger, orange zest, and cranberries. Simmer, stirring often, until berries pop (about 5 minutes). Stir in raisins, apples, and almonds. Cover and refrigerate. Serve at room temperature.

MAKES ABOUT 6 CUPS

Cranberry-Mandarin Orange Relish

3/4–1 cup sugar
1-3/4 cups water
1 (12-ounce) bag fresh cranberries, rinsed and drained
2 (11-ounce) cans mandarin oranges, drained
1 cup golden raisins
1/2 cup walnut pieces

Combine sugar and water, and bring to a boil over medium heat, stirring constantly. Add cranberries and oranges, and simmer over low heat until skins of berries begin to crack, stirring occasionally. Add raisins and simmer until raisins start to plump, stirring occasionally. Add walnut pieces and remove from heat. Allow to cool, then refrigerate in a sealed container until ready to serve.

MAKES ABOUT 6 CUPS

Part of this relish's appeal is that it comes together so easily—nothing to chop, mince, peel, or puree. Although 3/4 cup sugar is usually enough, Karen Zecy suggests the full 1 cup for a sweeter relish (which would also be delicious spooned over slabs of pound cake).

Sun-Dried Tomato Pesto

5 cups water
3/4 pound sun-dried tomatoes (not oil-packed)
8 cloves garlic, minced
1/2 cup extra-virgin olive oil
4 teaspoons balsamic vinegar
2 cups firmly packed basil or flat-leaf parsley
1-1/2 teaspoons honey
Freshly ground pepper to taste

Bring water to a boil and add tomatoes, making sure they are comfortably submerged. Reduce heat and simmer for 15 minutes, then drain and squeeze excess water from tomatoes. Whirl tomatoes and garlic in a food processor until mixture is coarsely chopped, stopping to scrape down sides occasionally. With machine running, gradually add oil and vinegar, and process for about 1 minute. Add basil, honey, and pepper, and whirl until thoroughly incorporated.

MAKES ABOUT 2 CUPS

Tucking a small jar of Linda Buchner's rich pesto into a basket of pasta and fresh Parmesan makes a much-appreciated remembrance for friends at the holidays. Linda inscribes the label as follows: "For a quick pasta sauce, add 2 to 3 tablespoons of reserved pasta cooking water to 1/4 cup pesto and toss with your favorite pasta."

Wild Mushroom Salsa

Like the relishes inspired by north-of-the-border traditions, "salsa" can signify either a cooked or fresh mixture. This one showcases an array of delectable mushrooms. As seasonal availability can affect your selection, also try this one with assorted dried mushrooms (soaked in warm water for 20 to 30 minutes, then rinsed well and drained before using).

1 tablespoon diced pancetta or smoked bacon
1/4 pound assorted fresh wild mushrooms, chopped
1 tablespoon chopped cilantro
1 serrano or jalapeño pepper, minced
1 tablespoon minced white onion
1/8 teaspoon salt

Sauté bacon until heated through but not browned (about 5 minutes). Add mushrooms and sauté over medium-high heat until soft and lightly browned (about 5 minutes more). Transfer mushrooms to a bowl, add remaining ingredients, toss, and serve.

MAKES ABOUT 1 CUP

Cranberry Salsa

Caroline McKnight discovered this berry salsa some years ago and now her family can't have Christmas without it. Not only does it do-si-do with just about any meat, in decorated jars it makes a standout hostess gift, too.

1 (12-ounce) bag fresh whole cranberries, rinsed and drained
2 jalapeño peppers, seeded and minced
1/4 cup chopped cilantro (or more to taste)
2 tablespoons diced onions
1/3 cup fresh lime juice
1/2 cup sugar
1/2 teaspoon salt
1/4 teaspoon freshly ground pepper

Cover cranberries with water, bring to a boil, and cook over medium-high heat for 2 minutes, just until most berries split. Drain well and transfer to plastic or glass container. Add remaining ingredients and combine thoroughly. Cover and refrigerate for up to 1 month.

MAKES ABOUT 2 CUPS

Christmas Pepper Jam

6–8 red or green bell peppers, coarsely chopped
2 tablespoons salt
1 cup red wine vinegar
1 cup sugar
Dash of Tabasco sauce or cayenne pepper
Red or green food coloring (optional)

Place peppers in a bowl and toss with salt. Cover with plastic wrap and leave overnight in a cool place. Drain off half the liquid and discard. Combine peppers, remaining liquid, vinegar, sugar, and Tabasco sauce, and bring to a boil. Reduce heat and simmer for 1 hour or until thickened, stirring occasionally. Add a few drops of food coloring if desired to brighten color. When thick, pour into sterilized jars and seal with paraffin wax or refrigerate. (Note: Keeps for 3 months in the refrigerator.)

MAKES ABOUT 2 CUPS

Condiments that reflect the colors of the holiday season make a pretty addition to any table. This red or green jam suits most holiday meals or entertaining occasions, and is a surefire hit as a gift from your kitchen.

Microwave Citrus Marmalade

1 navel orange
1 large lemon
1 large lime
1-1/2 cups sugar

Quarter fruits, taking care to remove seeds. Finely chop fruit pieces in a blender or food processor. Place in a glass bowl, add sugar, and mix well. Microwave on medium heat for about 5 to 6 minutes, stirring several times. Stored tightly covered in refrigerator.

MAKES ABOUT 2 CUPS

Busy lives can take a toll on family traditions such as preparing homemade jams and marmalades. Rather than abandoning these gracious touches, let the microwave and a few shortcuts help you take advantage of snatches of time.

Rosemary Orange Marmalade

9 sprigs fresh rosemary
2 cups boiling water
4–5 seedless oranges
3 cups sugar
3 ounces liquid pectin

Steep 5 sprigs of rosemary in boiling water for 30 minutes. Remove rosemary sprigs and discard, and reserve infused cooking liquid. Remove peel from orange and slice thin. Cover slices with water and simmer for 30 minutes. Drain and set aside. Remove membrane from orange sections and chop pulp. Put rosemary-infused water, orange peel, and chopped oranges in a nonaluminum pan. Bring to a boil, stirring, and then simmer for 35 minutes. Add pectin and boil for 1 minute. Place fresh sprigs of rosemary in 4 small sterilized jars and pour in marmalade. Refrigerate until ready to serve.

MAKES ABOUT 4 CUPS

Cardamom Pear Butter

Fruit butters are appealing cousins of jams and jellies, and offer a nice change in texture for familiar fruit spreads—apple, apricot, peach, grape, plum, and pear. Apple butter cooked with apple cider creates an especially nice flavor.

Winter pears
Sugar (1/2 cup per 1 cup fruit pulp)
Ground cardamom to taste

Wash pears, remove stems, and cut into fourths (do not peel or core). Place pear quarters in a pan with half as much water as fruit and simmer until fruit becomes soft, stirring frequently. Drain fruit and rub through a fine sieve or colander to remove fruit fibers and create a smooth consistency. Stir sugar into pulp (varying amount to taste) and return to pan. Bring mixture to a boil and cook until thick (and no rim of liquid appears when a small quantity is dropped onto a cold plate). Stir constantly while cooking to prevent burning. At the end of cooking period, stir in cardamom a little at a time, to taste. Ladle pear butter into hot sterilized jars while still boiling hot and seal tightly.

YIELD VARIES

CONDIMENTS

Jezebel Sauce

1 (18-ounce) jar pineapple preserves
1 (18-ounce) jar apple jelly
1 (2-1/2-ounce) jar prepared horseradish
1 (1-ounce) can dry mustard
1 teaspoon white pepper

Thoroughly combine all ingredients, pour into sterilized jars, and refrigerate for at least 4 hours before serving. (Note: Delicious with meats or as a spread with bagels and cream cheese. Keeps indefinitely in the refrigerator.)

MAKES ABOUT 5 CUPS

The name of this tangy sauce from JoAnn Dodson must refer to its sassy nature. The bite of horse-radish and hot mustard is mellowed by the sweet preserves, creating a condiment that marries well with a variety of meats or just cream cheese on a bagel.

Easy Kansas City BBQ Sauce

1/4 cup (1/2 stick) butter
2 onions, chopped
2 cups water
2 cups chili sauce
1/2 cup firmly packed brown sugar
1/4 cup plus 2 tablespoons Worcestershire sauce
1/4 cup herb vinegar
1 tablespoon dry mustard

Sauté onion in butter until tender. Stir in remaining ingredients and simmer for 15 minutes. Cool slightly and transfer to sterilized jars. Store tightly covered in refrigerator.

MAKES ABOUT 6 CUPS

A hallmark of Kansas City cuisine is barbecue sauce, all year-round and in every degree of tang. This simple version yields enough for several gifts—include a jar in a basket of 'que supplies, such as fruit wood chips and a tasty spice rub.

Maple Mustard

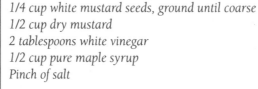

Hearty mustards are a must at holiday spreads, to serve with main dishes or on sandwiches scavenged from leftovers. There's an echo of rich maple in this first one.

1/4 cup white mustard seeds, ground until coarse
1/2 cup dry mustard
2 tablespoons white vinegar
1/2 cup pure maple syrup
Pinch of salt

Combine all ingredients, blend well, and pour into sterilized jars. Refrigerate tightly covered until ready to use. (Note: Excellent with ham, sausage, and pork).

MAKES ABOUT 1 CUP

Horseradish Mustard

Another traditional partner in mustard concoctions is bold horseradish. The warm taste in this combination definitely holds its own when served with hearty meats and cheeses.

1/2 cup dry mustard
1/8 teaspoon white pepper
1 teaspoon salt
1 teaspoon firmly packed brown sugar
1 clove garlic, minced
1/2 cup white wine vinegar
1–2 tablespoons prepared horseradish
1/4 cup water

Sift together mustard, pepper, salt, and brown sugar. Add remaining ingredients and blend well. Simmer over low heat, stirring until thickened. (If mixture becomes too thick, thin with additional water or vinegar). Pour into sterilized jars and refrigerate until ready to use. (Note: Good with hearty fare like beef, ham, and sausages.)

MAKES ABOUT 1 CUP

Breads

Coffee Cakes, Breads,
Muffins, & Rolls

Mrs. Novosel's Povetica

2 packages active dry yeast
1/4 cup plus 1/2 teaspoon sugar
1/2 cup lukewarm water
2 cups lukewarm milk
2 teaspoons salt
7 cups all-purpose flour
1/3 cup vegetable oil, plus additional

FILLING:
1-1/2 cups milk
1 cup (2 sticks) butter
2 pounds walnuts, ground
6 eggs
3 cups sugar

Diane Garrett supplied this version of a Croatian specialty, the recipe for which originated with her children's great-grand-mother. Karen Adler's grandmother, who was born in Josep, Yugoslavia, also fixed povetica every year for the holidays. Kansas Citians interested in all sorts of Slavic goodies can take classes at the Strawberry Hill Museum and Cultural Center.

Soften yeast and 1/2 teaspoon sugar in lukewarm water. Combine remaining 1/4 cup sugar, milk, salt, and 3 cups flour (1 cup at a time). Stir in oil, yeast mixture, and remaining flour (1 cup at a time) to form a sticky dough. Divide dough in half, place pieces on a well-floured surface, and knead for 15 to 20 minutes. Place each dough half in a large oiled bowl, cover with a damp cloth, and let rise in a warm place until doubled in bulk (about 2 hours).

To make filling, scald milk and butter over low heat in a heavy pan (filling burns easily). Add nuts, eggs, and sugar, stirring constantly. Cook over low heat for about 5 minutes, then remove from heat and cool thoroughly before spreading on dough.

Preheat oven to 350 degrees. Grease two 9-inch square baking pans. Cover a large table with a cloth larger than the table (a sheet will do). Lightly flour cloth, then place raised dough halves in the center. Roll out dough to a little larger than "pie size," spread some oil on top for elasticity. Begin pulling dough from the center to the outside edges. Dough should be oval shaped and paper-thin when done (it may tear, but that's OK). Spread half the filling on each piece of dough evenly but thinly, covering completely. Trim off outside edge so that dough is of uniform thickness. Form each dough oval into a roll by lifting the end of the cloth and rolling dough evenly over and over (do not work too rapidly). Put rolls into prepared pans, forming an "S" shape (be sure that the parts of the "S" are pushed closely together). Bake for 40 minutes, then reduce oven temperature to 325 degrees and bake for 20 minutes more. Cool before slicing.

MAKES 2 LOAVES

Dresden Stollen

This traditional German yeast bread is a favorite breakfast item in the Conde household at holiday time. Slice and serve it plain or with jam (it's also delicious toasted).

2 packages active dry yeast
1/2 cup warm water
1-1/4 cups buttermilk
2 eggs
5-1/2 cups all-purpose flour
1/2 cup (1 stick) butter, softened
1/2 cup sugar
2 teaspoons baking powder
2 teaspoons salt
1/2 cup chopped pecans
1 tablespoon dried grated lemon peel
1 cup chopped mixed candied fruit
1/2 cup confectioners' sugar dissolved in 1 tablespoon milk

Dissolve yeast in water, then add buttermilk, eggs, 2-1/2 cups flour, butter, sugar, baking powder, and salt. Beat on low speed for 30 seconds, scraping sides and bottom of bowl, then beat on medium speed for 2 minutes more. Stir in remaining flour, pecans, lemon peel, and candied fruit (dough should remain soft and slightly sticky). Knead for 5 minutes on a lightly floured board, then roll out to a 24-by-6-inch strip. Cut into 3 lengths (each 24 inches by 2 inches) and loosely braid and pinch ends. Place on a greased baking sheet and let rise in a warm place until doubled in bulk (about 1 hour). Preheat oven to 375 degrees. Bake for 30 minutes. Let cool for 15 minutes, then brush with glaze of confectioners' sugar and milk.

SERVES 20

Buñuelos with Cinnamon-Wine Sauce

In Mexico, these large "doughnuts" are a traditional sweet of the Christmas season. Buñuelos are often served on cheap pottery plates so that afterward diners can smash their plates to the ground in a fun gesture to invoke good luck.

4 cups all-purpose flour
2 tablespoons sugar
1 teaspoon baking powder
1/2 teaspoon salt
1 cup milk
1 large egg
1 teaspoon anise seeds, crushed
3–4 cups vegetable oil

SAUCE:
3/4 cup dry red wine
1/3 cup brown sugar
1/2 cup raisins
1/2 teaspoon ground cinnamon

Sift together flour, sugar, baking powder, and salt. Whisk milk and egg together until frothy, then stir in anise. Stir milk mixture into flour mixture, making a dough. Remove dough to a lightly floured surface and knead lightly until smooth and satiny (about 5 to 10 minutes). Divide dough into approximately 30 pieces and shape into balls. Cover with a cloth and let stand for 20 minutes. On a lightly floured surface, roll each ball out into a circle about the size of a tortilla. Heat oil to 360 degrees. Fry circles of dough a few at time for 3 to 5 minutes, turning once, until golden brown and puffy. Drain on paper towels. To make sauce, heat wine, sugar, raisins, and cinnamon. Simmer, stirring, until sugar dissolves completely. Spoon over buñuelos.

MAKES ABOUT 2-1/2 DOZEN

Panettone

2 packages active dry yeast
1 cup warm water
4-1/2 cups all-purpose flour
1/2 cup (1 stick) butter, softened, plus 1 tablespoon, melted
1/2 cup sugar
3 large eggs
2 teaspoons dried grated lemon peel
2 teaspoons dried grated orange peel
1/2 teaspoon salt
1/2 cup unblanched almonds, sliced
1/4 cup chopped citron
1/4 cup dark raisins

Dissolve yeast in warm water for about 5 minutes. Beat in 1 cup flour, then cover and let rise until double in bulk (about 1 hour). Cream butter and sugar, then beat in eggs 1 at a time. Add citrus peels and salt. Stir down yeast mixture and then add to butter mixture. Add remaining flour, almonds, and fruit. Put dough in a large greased bowl and turn to grease top and sides. Cover and let rise for about 1-1/2 hours, or until doubled again. Punch dough down and divide in half. Grease two 1-pound coffee cans and put 1 piece of dough in each. Cover with plastic wrap and let dough rise over tops of cans. Preheat oven to 350 degrees. Brush tops of dough with 1 tablespoon melted butter. Bake for 30 to 40 minutes until browned and loaves sound hollow when tapped. Cool, then remove from pans.

MAKES 2 LOAVES

A delicious symbol of the Italian Christmas is festive panettone. Serve it warm, cold, or toasted and spread with creamy butter.

Grandma Pearson's Rye Bread

Calvert Guthrie's Swedish grandma, Anna Pearson, was a wonderful cook. One of her specialties was fragrant rye bread, scrumptious with butter and sweet toppings or as the start of a thick ham sandwich.

1/2 cup vegetable shortening
3 cups warm water
1 tablespoon salt
1 cup firmly packed brown sugar
1/2 cup dark corn syrup
1 tablespoon plus 2 teaspoons dried grated orange peel
1 tablespoon plus 2 teaspoons anise seeds
3 cups rye flour
All-purpose flour
2 packages yeast

Melt shortening and add to 2 cups warm water, along with salt, sugar, and corn syrup. Dissolve yeast in remaining warm water. When shortening mixture has cooled, add yeast mixture. Stir in orange peel and anise seeds, followed by rye flour and enough all-purpose flour to make a stiff dough. Knead well and let rise twice, punching down after each. Preheat oven to 350 degrees and grease three 9-by-5-inch loaf pans. Divide dough into thirds and place in prepared pans. Bake for about 45 minutes. Cool before slicing.

MAKES 3 LOAVES

Prune-Apricot Coffee Cake

Although its origins are long forgotten, this recipe has been a standard Christmas morning brunch item for nearly 30 years at Vicki Johnson's house. She recommends it with fruit platters and various egg dishes.

3/4 cup dried pitted prunes
3/4 cup dried apricots
Hot water
2 cups plus 1 tablespoon all-purpose flour
2 teaspoons baking powder
1/2 teaspoon salt
2/3 cup firmly packed brown sugar
1 tablespoon ground cinnamon
3/4 cup vegetable shortening
3/4 cup sugar
2 eggs
3/4 milk
1 teaspoon vanilla extract
1/4 cup plus 2 tablespoons butter or margarine, melted
1/3 cup chopped walnuts

Preheat oven to 350 degrees. Lightly grease and flour a 9-inch tube pan. Cover prunes and apricots with hot water, let stand for 5 minutes, and then drain and chop fine. Sift together 2 cups flour, baking powder, and salt. Combine brown sugar, 1 table-spoon flour, and cinnamon. Cream shortening and sugar until mixture is light and fluffy. Add eggs 1 at a time, beating after each addition. Beat in flour mixture one-third a time, alternating with milk and vanilla. Gently fold in fruit. Turn one-third of batter into prepared pan, spreading evenly. Sprinkle with one-third of brown sugar mixture, and then 2 tablespoons butter. Repeat twice. Sprinkle top with nuts. Bake for about 50 minutes, or until done. Cool in pan on wire rack for 15 to 20 minutes before removing.

SERVES 8–10

Sour Cream Coffee Cake

1/2 cup vegetable shortening
3/4 cup sugar
1 teaspoon vanilla extract
3 eggs
2 cups sifted all-purpose flour
2 teaspoons salt
1 teaspoon baking powder
1 teaspoon baking soda
1 cup sour cream

TOPPING:
1/4 cup plus 2 tablespoons butter or margarine, chilled and cubed
1 cup firmly packed brown sugar
2 teaspoons ground cinnamon
1 tablespoon all-purpose flour
1 cup chopped nuts (walnuts or pecans)

Preheat oven to 350 degrees. Grease and flour a 10-inch tube pan. Cut together all topping ingredients until mixture becomes crumbly, then set aside. Cream shortening, sugar, and vanilla thoroughly. Add eggs 1 at a time, beating after each addition. Sift together flour, salt, baking powder, and baking soda. Add to creamed mixture alternating with sour cream, blending well after each addition. Spread half of batter into prepared pan, then sprinkle half of topping mixture evenly over batter in pan. Cover with remaining batter and sprinkle on remaining topping. Bake for 50 minutes or until done. Cool a bit before slicing.

SERVES 8–10

Marcia Hamilton's mother always made this coffee cake for Christmas breakfast (and for birthdays, too, at other times of the year). Now that all the kids are grown and gone, she gives each of them a coffee cake at Christmastime.

Mincemeat Crumb Coffee Cake

Often there's a little mincemeat left over after baking holiday pies. Rather than just sticking it in the refrigerator (and then throwing it out in February), try this yummy way to greet the morning.

1-1/2 cups all-purpose flour
1/2 cup sugar
2 teaspoons baking powder
1/2 teaspoon salt
1 egg
1/2 cup milk
3 tablespoons butter or margarine, melted and cooled
1 cup prepared mincemeat

TOPPING:
2 tablespoons all-purpose flour
1/4 cup sugar
1-1/2 teaspoons ground cinnamon
2 tablespoons butter or margarine, chilled and cubed

Preheat oven to 400 degrees. Grease a 9-inch round cake pan. For topping, stir together dry ingredients and then cut in butter until mixture becomes crumbly. Set aside. Stir together flour, sugar, baking powder, and salt. Beat egg with milk and melted butter. Add egg mixture to flour mixture, stirring until mixture is smooth. Fold in mincemeat. Spread batter into prepared pan and sprinkle with topping. Bake for about 25 to 30 minutes, or until a tester inserted comes out clean. Serve warm or at room temperature.

SERVES 6–8

Shortcut Coffee Ring

Karen Zecy prepares this easy coffee ring the night before so she can serve it with a breakfast casserole on Christmas Day. Sometimes she makes it look like a wreath, other times it becomes a candy cane instead.

1/2 (32-ounce) package frozen bread dough, thawed
3 tablespoons butter or margarine, softened
1-1/3 cups sifted confectioners' sugar
1/2 teaspoon vanilla extract
1/2 cup pecans
1/4 cup raisins
1/2 finely chopped apple (optional)
2 tablespoons milk

Roll dough into a 14-by-8-inch strip on a lightly floured surface. Cream butter with 1/3 cup sugar and vanilla, then spread over dough, leaving a 1-inch margin. Sprinkle on nuts, raisins, and apple if desired, also leaving the margin. Roll up jelly-roll style, starting at long side, then pinch seam to seal. Place on a greased baking sheet (seam-side down), shape into a ring, and pinch ends together to seal. Using kitchen shears, make cuts in dough every inch around ring, cutting two-thirds through the roll at each cut. Gently turn each cut piece to one side, slightly overlapping slices. Cover and let rise for 45 minutes, or until doubled in bulk. Preheat oven to 350 degrees. Bake on lower oven rack for 20 to 25 minutes. Transfer to a wire rack. Combine remaining sugar and milk, then drizzle over ring while still warm.

SERVES 8–10

Cranberry-Apricot Oat Bread

2 cups all-purpose flour
1 cup oats (quick or old-fashioned), uncooked
1 cup sugar
2 teaspoons baking powder
1/2 teaspoon baking soda
3/4 teaspoon salt (optional)
2 eggs
1/2 cup vegetable oil
1/2 cup orange juice
1/3 cup water
1 tablespoon grated fresh orange zest
3/4 cup chopped fresh cranberries
1/2 cup finely chopped dried apricots
1/2 cup chopped nuts

Preheat oven to 350 degrees. Grease and flour bottom only of a 9-by-5-inch loaf pan. Combine flour, oats, sugar, baking powder, baking soda, and salt, mixing well. Beat eggs and oil thoroughly, then mix in orange juice, water, and orange zest. Add to dry ingredients, mixing just until moistened. Stir in cranberries, apricots, and nuts, mixing evenly. Bake for 1 hour or until a tester inserted comes out clean. Cool for 10 minutes in pan, then remove to a wire rack to finishing cooling completely.

MAKES 1 LOAF

Dee Conde's recipe files seem to overflow with wonderful breads. She varies this one by using candied cherries in lieu of the cranberries and lemon peel instead of the orange, plus she'll toss in a half cup of dates, too.

Date-Pecan Loaf

Angie Stout brought this recipe along when she moved to Kansas City from Memphis. It's a reliable "do-ahead" item that also freezes well. If you have a date nut bread you want to dress up a little, substitute 1/4 cup of Marsala wine for some of the liquid in the batter.

1 cup sugar
4 eggs, well beaten
1 teaspoon vanilla extract
1 cup sifted all-purpose flour
1 teaspoon salt
2 teaspoon baking powder
1 pound pecans, chopped
1 pound dates, chopped

Preheat oven to 325 degrees. Grease two 9-by-5-inch loaf pans. Gradually mix together sugar with eggs and vanilla. Combine flour, salt, and baking powder, sift three times, and then add to egg mixture. Alternately stir pecans and dates into batter. Pour batter into prepared pans and bake for 1 hour or until a tester inserted comes out clean. Cool before slicing.

MAKES 2 LOAVES

Red-and-White Gift Loaves

Mini loaves loaded with "special occasion" ingredients make charming inclusions in parcels of giftable goodies. This recipe also yields one 9-by-5-inch full-sized loaf.

2 cups all-purpose flour
1/2 cup sugar
2 teaspoons baking powder
1/2 teaspoon salt
3/4 cup milk, room temperature
1/3 cup unsalted butter, melted and cooled
1 egg, room temperature, lightly beaten
1-1/2 teaspoons vanilla extract
1 cup dried cranberries
3/4 cup white chocolate chips

Preheat oven to 350 degrees. Grease 4 mini loaf pans. Combine flour, sugar, baking powder, and salt. Stir together milk, butter, egg, and vanilla, blending well. Make a well in the center of flour mixture and add milk mixture, stirring just to combine. Fold in cranberries and white chocolate pieces. Pour batter into prepared pans and spread evenly. Bake for about 40 minutes, or until a tester inserted comes out clean. Cool in pans for 10 minutes on a wire rack, then turn out onto rack to finish cooling. Store in air-tight containers in the refrigerator (serve at room temperature).

MAKES 4 MINI LOAVES

Rum Raisin Bread

1/2 cup golden raisins
1/2 cup currants
Grated zest of 1 large lemon
1/2 cup dark rum
1 teaspoon vanilla extract
2 cups all-purpose flour
3/4 cup sugar
2 teaspoons baking powder
1/2 teaspoon baking soda
1/2 teaspoon salt
1/4 teaspoon grated nutmeg
2 eggs
1/2 cup sour cream or plain yogurt
1/4 cup (1/2 stick) butter, melted
Confectioners' sugar (optional)

Preheat oven to 350 degrees. Grease a 9-by-5-inch loaf pan. Combine raisins, currants, lemon zest, rum, and vanilla, and let stand for 30 minutes. Mix together flour, sugar, baking powder, baking soda, salt, and nutmeg. Stir eggs, sour cream, and butter into raisin mixture, and blend well. Pour mixture over dry ingredients and fold in just until combined. Spoon batter into prepared pan and smooth on top. Place on oven rack in top third position and bake for 60 to 75 minutes, or until a tester inserted comes out clean. Turn out onto rack and dust top with sugar. Allow to cool.

MAKES 1 LOAF

For brunch, tea, or just a "pick me up" after Christmas shopping, try this delicious bread toasted. As you'll see when you make it, even the batter is wonderfully aromatic.

Banana Nut Bread

1/2 cup vegetable shortening
1 cup sugar
2 eggs, beaten
3 bananas, mashed
1 teaspoon salt
1/2 teaspoon baking soda
1-1/2 teaspoons baking powder
2 cups all-purpose flour
3 tablespoons sour cream liquid (1 teaspoon vinegar in milk)
1 tablespoon fresh lemon juice
1 cup chopped nuts

Preheat oven to 350 degrees. Grease a 9-by-5-inch loaf pan. Cream together shortening and sugar, then add eggs and bananas, followed by remaining ingredients. Bake for 1 hour or until a tester inserted comes out clean. Cool before slicing.

MAKES 1 LOAF

This tasty bread is a point of pride for Dee Conde— even she concedes it's the best ever.

Herbed Parmesan Streusel Bread

For casual occasions such as soup, salad, and bread buffets, this dense savory loaf is always a hit. The cheesy crumbles on top present a delightful invitation to nibble.

2 cups all-purpose flour
1 tablespoon sugar
2 teaspoons baking powder
1/2 teaspoon salt
1/2 cup milk, room temperature
1/2 cup (1 stick) unsalted butter, melted and cooled
2 eggs, room temperature

FILLING/TOPPING:
3/4 cup freshly grated Parmesan cheese
1/2 teaspoon dried basil
1/2 teaspoon dried oregano
1/4 cup all-purpose flour
2–3 tablespoons unsalted butter, chilled and cubed

Preheat oven to 350 degrees. Grease a 9-by-5-inch loaf pan. To prepare filling/topping, combine Parmesan, herbs, and flour, and transfer to a food processor. Sprinkle butter cubes onto cheese mixture and pulse until mixture resembles coarse crumbs. Set aside. For bread, stir together flour, sugar, baking powder, and salt. Combine milk, butter, and eggs. Make a well in the center of flour mixture and pour in liquid mixture, stirring just to combine. Spoon half of batter into prepared pan and spread evenly, then top with half of Parmesan-herb mixture. Evenly spoon remaining batter over filling and then top with remaining cheese mixture. Bake for 40 to 50 minutes, or until bread begins to brown and a tester inserted comes out clean. Cool in pan for 10 minutes, then turn out onto a wire rack and finish cooling completely before storing in an airtight container.

MAKES 1 LOAF

Cheesy Bruschetta-Spread Bread

This quick-to-assemble loaf accompanies meat entrees well, but it also can be enjoyed as an hors d'oeuvre.

1 loaf French bread
1 (4-1/2-ounce) can black olives, drained
1 (4-ounce) can chopped green chilies, drained
1 (8-ounce) can tomato sauce
3–4 cloves garlic, minced
2 cups grated sharp cheddar cheese
1/4 cup grated Romano cheese

Slice bread lengthwise. Combine remaining ingredients and spread onto cut surface of bread. Broil until mixture is bubbly, then cut into serving pieces.

SERVES 8–10

Jalapeño Corn Bread

1 cup cornmeal
1 tablespoon sugar
1/2 tablespoon baking powder
1 teaspoon salt
2 eggs, beaten
1/2 cup vegetable oil
1 (16-ounce) can creamed corn
1 large onion, diced
2 cups grated cheddar cheese
1/4 cup jalapeño pepper, seeded and chopped
2 tablespoons chopped pimiento
1 clove garlic, minced
Tabasco sauce to taste

Preheat oven to 400 degrees. Grease a 9-by-12-inch baking pan. Combine all ingredients, then pour into prepared pan. Bake for 35 minutes, or until a tester inserted comes out clean.

SERVES 8–10

Spicy squares of corn cake make delicious partners for pork or poultry as well as hearty bean soups. This recipe is also fine, though, as a brunch item.

Crunchy Double-Pumpkin Muffins

2 cups all-purpose flour
3/4 cup firmly packed brown sugar
2 teaspoons baking powder
1/4 teaspoon baking soda
1/2 teaspoon salt
1 teaspoon ground cinnamon
1/4 teaspoon ground ginger
1/8 teaspoon ground cloves
Dash of ground nutmeg
1 cup canned pumpkin
1/3 cup butter, melted and cooled
2 eggs, room temperature
1/4 cup buttermilk, room temperature
2 teaspoons vanilla extract
1/2 cup raw pumpkin seeds

Preheat oven to 400 degrees. Lightly grease 3 mini muffin tins. Stir together flour, sugar, baking powder, baking soda, salt, and spices. Combine pumpkin, butter, eggs, buttermilk, and vanilla. Make a well in the center of flour mixture and pour in pumpkin mixture. Stir until just combined. Fold in pumpkin seeds. Spoon batter into prepared tins and bake for 15 to 20 minutes, or until a tester inserted comes out clean. Cool in tins for 5 minutes, then turn out onto wire racks.

MAKES ABOUT 3 DOZEN

The rich green pepitas studding these golden muffins offer textural as well as visual appeal. As an option, sprinkle the tops with sugar before baking to give the muffins a nice crunchy surface.

Refrigerator Bran Muffins

Because the batter stores so well in the refrigerator, don't overlook this humble combination when searching for "kitchen gift" ideas. In a pretty glass jar with a plaid bow and nicely lettered instructions, this can be a warm remembrance for special neighbors.

1 cup boiling water
1 cup Nabisco 100% Bran cereal
1-1/2 cups sugar
1/2 cup vegetable shortening
2 beaten eggs
2-1/2 cups all-purpose flour
2-1/2 teaspoons baking soda
1/2 teaspoon salt
2 cups Kelloggs All Bran cereal
1 cup chopped dates (optional)

Preheat oven to 400 degrees. Grease muffin tins well. Pour boiling water over 100% bran and let stand for 3 to 4 minutes. Cream together sugar and shortening, then add eggs and bran mixture. Sift together flour, baking soda, and salt, then fold along with All Bran and dates into creamed mixture just until blended. Bake for 20 minutes, or store batter in a tightly covered container in the refrigerator for up to 1 week.

MAKES ABOUT 1-1/2 DOZEN

"Spirited" Chocolate Muffins

These deliciously light and gently crunchy muffins resemble airy brownies somewhat. Two bites and they're gone.

3/4 cup all-purpose flour
1/2 teaspoon baking soda
1/4 teaspoon salt
1/2 cup (1 stick) lightly salted butter, softened
1/2 cup sugar
1 ounce good-quality semisweet chocolate, melted
1 egg
1 tablespoon full-flavored sherry or bourbon
1 teaspoon vanilla extract
1/2 cup semisweet mini chocolate chips
1/2 cup chopped pecans
Pecan halves

Preheat oven to 400 degrees. Lightly grease 3 mini muffin tins. Combine flour, baking soda, and salt. Cream together butter and sugar until light and fluffy, then beat in chocolate, egg, sherry, and vanilla. Add dry ingredients and stir just to combine, then fold in chocolate chips and pecans. Spoon batter into prepared tins (fill about two-thirds full), top with pecan halves, and bake for 15 to 20 minutes, or a tester inserted comes out clean. Cool in tins for 5 minutes, then turn out onto wire racks.

MAKES ABOUT 3 DOZEN

Yogurt Pound Cake Muffins

1-3/4 cups all-purpose flour
1/4 teaspoon baking soda
1/2 teaspoon salt
3/4 cup sugar
1/2 cup (1 stick) lightly salted butter, softened
1/2 cup plain yogurt
1/2 teaspoon ground mace
2 eggs

Preheat oven to 400 degrees. Grease 3 mini muffin tins. Combine flour, baking soda, and salt. Cream sugar and butter until well combined, then add yogurt and mace, followed by eggs (1 at a time). Stir in dry ingredients just until combined. Spoon batter into prepared tins and bake for 15 to 20 minutes, or until a tester inserted comes out clean. Cool in tins for 5 minutes, then turn out onto wire racks.

MAKES ABOUT 3 DOZEN

These sunny little muffins are heady with mace. They're terrific with jams and jellies as well as with shavings of sweet cured ham.

Almond-Raspberry Macaroon Muffins

1 (8-ounce) can almond paste
About 6 tablespoons seedless raspberry jam
2 cups all-purpose flour
2/3 cup sugar
2 teaspoons baking powder
1/2 teaspoon salt
1 cup milk
1/2 cup (1 stick) lightly salted butter, melted and cooled
1 egg, lightly beaten
1 teaspoon vanilla extract
1/4 teaspoon almond extract
3/4 cup flaked coconut
Finely chopped almonds

Preheat oven to 400 degrees. Lightly grease 3 mini muffin tins. Roll out almond paste to about 1/8-inch thick and, with a 1-1/4-inch canape cutter, cut out 72 pieces. Dab half of cutouts with jam, then top with remaining cutouts. Press edges to seal. Stir together flour, sugar, baking powder, and salt. Combine milk, butter, egg, and extracts. Make a well in center of flour mixture, then add liquid ingredients and stir just to combine. Fold in coconut. Spoon half of batter into prepared tins, then place a jam-filled "pocket" in center of each, and then spoon in remaining batter. Top with almonds. Bake for 15 to 20 minutes, or until light brown. Cool in tins for 5 minutes, then turn out onto wire racks.

MAKES 3 DOZEN

Biting into these wee treats produces a delectable surprise—a raspberry "marzipan" center. These muffins make outstanding teatime goodies and enchanting gifts for special friends.

Hot Cherry Scones

Sweet scones are much appreciated when shared with fellow Anglophiles. For an "atmospheric" gift, wrap and nestle some of these in a basket along with packets of flavored tea and a pair of pretty cups.

2 cups all-purpose flour
2 teaspoons baking powder
1/2 teaspoon baking soda
1/4 teaspoon salt
2 tablespoons sugar
1 teaspoon dried grated lemon peel
1/2 cup (1 stick) butter or margarine, chilled and cubed
1/2 cup dried cherries
1/4 cup buttermilk

Preheat oven to 425 degrees. Combine first 6 ingredients, then cut in butter with a pastry blender until mixture becomes crumbly. Add cherries, tossing lightly. Add buttermilk, stirring until dry ingredients are just moistened. Turn dough out onto a lightly floured surface and knead lightly 6 times. Divide dough in half. Shape each portion into a 7-inch circle on an ungreased baking sheet, then cut each circle into 6 wedges. Bake for 10 minutes. Cool on wire racks.

MAKES 1 DOZEN

Sweet Potato Biscuits

Among the many nice things about biscuits is how easy they are to make. Just remember to keep your touch light when blending the dry and liquid ingredients. This recipe produces tasty partners for country ham.

2 medium sweet potatoes, baked, peeled, and mashed
1/4 cup firmly packed brown sugar
3 cups all-purpose flour
1-1/2 tablespoons baking powder
1/2 teaspoon salt
1 teaspoon ground cinnamon
1/2 teaspoon ground nutmeg
1/2 teaspoon ground mace
1 teaspoon dried grated lemon peel
1 cup (2 sticks) unsalted butter, chilled and cubed
1/4 cup milk

Preheat oven to 450 degrees. Puree sweet potato pulp with sugar until smooth. Sift together flour, baking powder, salt, and spices, then mix in lemon peel. Cut in butter with a pastry blender until mixture resembles coarse meal. Add puree and milk, and stir until just blended. Gather into a ball, turn out onto a lightly floured surface, and knead 2 or 3 times. Flatten to a thickness of 3/4 inch. Cut out biscuits with a 3-inch cutter lightly dipped in flour. Prick tops with a fork, then arrange 1/2 inch apart on an ungreased baking sheet. Bake for 12 to 15 minutes, or until golden brown.

MAKES ABOUT 1-1/2 DOZEN

Savory Sage-Dijon Biscuits

2 cups all-purpose flour
1 tablespoon baking powder
1/2 teaspoon salt
1/4 teaspoon rubbed sage
1/4 cup plus 2 tablespoons vegetable shortening, cubed
1/2 cup plus 2 tablespoons cold milk, plus additional to brush tops
    of biscuits
2 tablespoons country-style Dijon mustard

Preheat oven to 400 degrees. Lightly grease a large heavy baking sheet. Combine flour, baking powder, salt, and sage in a food processor and whirl for 5 seconds. Add shortening and pulse until mixture becomes crumbly. Transfer to a bowl. Whisk together milk and mustard, then gradually pour over flour mixture and stir just until moistened. Turn mixture out onto a floured surface and knead gently, just until dough comes together. Roll out to a thickness of 1/2 inch, then cut out biscuits with a 2-inch cutter. Gather scraps, roll out again, and cut out additional rounds. Place biscuits 1 inch apart on prepared sheet, then brush tops with milk. Bake in center of oven for about 14 minutes, or until light golden. Serve hot.

MAKES ABOUT 1-1/2 DOZEN

Mustard and sage so often lace heavier dishes, it's a pleasant surprise when the taste buds find them in these flaky biscuits. The flavors complement either meat or poultry well.

Orange-Pecan-Scallion Biscuits

2-1/2 cups all-purpose flour
2 tablespoons sugar
1 teaspoon dried grated orange peel
1/2 teaspoon baking soda
1/2 teaspoon salt
1/2 cup (1 stick) unsalted butter, chilled and cubed
1 cup toasted chopped pecans
1 teaspoon finely minced scallions
1 cup buttermilk, plus additional to brush tops of biscuits

Preheat oven to 425 degrees. Combine flour, sugar, orange peel, baking soda, and salt. Add butter and blend with fingertips until mixture resembles coarse meal. Mix in pecans, scallions, and buttermilk, and stir just until dough forms. Transfer mixture to a floured surface and pat out to a 3/4-inch-thick circle. Cut into rounds with a 2-inch cutter. Transfer rounds to ungreased baking sheets, brush tops with buttermilk, and bake until golden brown (about 18 minutes).

MAKES ABOUT 1-1/2 DOZEN

Although just plain old biscuits rarely disappoint, "dressier" versions can perch proudly on holiday tables. Jane Guthrie used a leaf-shaped cookie cutter for these one year and it made a pretty sight.

Pleasing Popovers

Popovers sometimes acquire a reputation as temperamental little creations, but it's largely ill-deserved (and probably the result of impatient cooks who peek too soon). The ingredients here are few and basic; just make sure that your measurements are accurate.

1 cup sifted all-purpose flour
1/4 teaspoon salt
1 teaspoon sugar (optional)
1 tablespoon melted butter
1 cup milk
2 eggs

Preheat oven to 400 degrees. Grease 12 muffin cups (1/3-cup size). Combine flour with salt and sugar, then add butter, milk, and eggs, beating at medium-high speed until mixture becomes very smooth (scrape bowl frequently with a rubber spatula). Fill prepared cups about half full, and bake on center rack for about 40 minutes, or until popovers are well browned and firm to the touch (keep oven door closed until finished—popovers are susceptible to collapse as they bake and swell). Serve hot.

MAKES 1 DOZEN

Melt-in-Your-Mouth Dropped Rolls

Inspired by Janet Ida of Fort Scott, Kansas, these homey "bites" are tasty partners for an entree of wild game or Missouri catfish.

1 cup (2 sticks) butter, softened
2 cups self-rising flour
1 cup sour cream
Snipped fresh or dried herbs (such as chives) to taste

Preheat oven to 350 degrees. Grease a baking sheet and set aside. Cut butter into flour, and then stir sour cream and herbs into mixture. Drop dough by rounded spoonfuls onto prepared sheet and bake for 20 minutes, or until rolls are firm (they will not brown). Serve warm.

MAKES ABOUT 2-1/2 DOZEN

Desserts

Hot, Cold,
Frozen, & Sauces

Persimmon Pudding

1/4 cup brandy
1/4 cup golden raisins
1/4 cup currants
3 tablespoons unsalted butter, softened
1 cup sugar
2 large eggs, separated
1 teaspoon vanilla extract
2 teaspoons fresh lemon juice
2–3 very ripe persimmons
3/4 cup half-and-half
1 teaspoon baking soda
1 tablespoon hot water
1-1/4 cups all-purpose flour
1-1/2 teaspoons ground cinnamon
1/2 teaspoon ground nutmeg
1/4 teaspoon salt
3/4 cup coarsely chopped pecans, toasted

Grease an 8-cup lidded pudding mold and set aside. In a small saucepan over low heat, combine brandy, raisins, and currants, and bring to a simmer. Remove from heat and let sit for 15 minutes. With an electric mixer, cream together butter and sugar. Beat in egg yolks, vanilla, and lemon juice. Cut tops off persimmons. Scoop out pulp and push through a strainer (discarding seeds and skins), then combine with half-and-half. Dissolve baking soda in hot water, add to egg mixture, and then add egg mixture to persimmons. Sift together flour, spices, and salt, and add to persimmon mixture, beating just until combined. Stir in pecans. In another bowl, beat egg whites until stiff peaks form, then fold into batter.

Pour into mold over raisins and currants, and clamp on lid. Place a wire rack or folded dish towel in the bottom of a pan that is large enough to hold the mold and provide a 2-inch clearance on all sides. Fill with enough water to reach halfway up sides of mold. Cover pan and bring to a boil, then turn down to a simmer. Place mold on rack in pot, replace cover and steam pudding for 2 hours and 20 minutes. Add boiling water as necessary to maintain water level. Remove mold from pot and let cool, uncovered, for 15 minutes before serving. (Note: As a serving option, warm 1/4 cup of brandy, pour over pudding, and ignite.)

SERVES 8–10

Ginny Beall used to fix traditional plum pudding for Christmas Day, but then the family fell in love with this one from her husband Scott's family in California. Don't forget the hard sauce!

English Plum Pudding with Hard Sauce

This is the perfect finale to an old-fashioned English feast. One Christmas Ginny Beall and a friend adapted this recipe for miniature plum puddings and distributed them with portions of hard sauce to neighbors and other special people on their lists.

1-1/2 cups seedless raisins
1/2 cup dried currants
1/2 cup finely chopped mixed candied fruit
1 tart apple, peeled, cored, and grated finely
1 lemon rind, grated finely
1 orange rind, grated finely
3/4 cup ale or orange juice
1 cup sifted all-purpose flour
1 teaspoon baking powder
1/2 teaspoon salt
1 teaspoon ground cinnamon
1/2 teaspoon ground allspice
1/4 teaspoon ground nutmeg
1 cup fine dry bread crumbs
1 cup firmly packed dark brown sugar
1/3 cup molasses
1 cup finely ground suet (available from butcher)
3 eggs, lightly beaten
1/2 cup minced toasted almonds

SAUCE:
1/2 cup (1 stick) butter, softened
2 cups sifted confectioners' sugar
1/8 teaspoon salt
1 teaspoon water
1 tablespoon hot water
1 tablespoon brandy

Thoroughly grease a large pudding mold (or two 1-quart molds). Mix fruits, rinds, and ale, and let stand for 30 minutes. Sift flour with baking powder, salt, and spices, then stir in remaining ingredients, add fruit mixture, and mix well. Spoon batter into prepared mold, cover with a double thickness of foil, and tie foil firmly in place. Set on a rack in a large pan, add boiling water to come halfway up mold, then cover pan and steam for 4 hours (keep water simmering slowly and add more boiling water as needed to maintain level). Cool puddings on rack with foil still intact, then store in a cool place, freeze, or refrigerate. (To reheat, steam for 1 hour in the same manner as cooking.)

To make sauce, beat butter until creamy, then gradually add sugar. Add remaining ingredients and continue to beat until fluffy. Refrigerate sauce if not using immediately (serve chilled or at room temperature). Unmold pudding onto a hot platter and decorate if desired. Cut into wedges and serve with hard sauce.

SERVES 12

Sugarplum Pudding

2 cups sifted all-purpose flour
2-1/2 teaspoons baking powder
1/2 teaspoon salt
1-1/2 cups sugar
1-1/4 teaspoons soda
1 teaspoon ground nutmeg
1 teaspoon ground allspice
1 cup chopped nuts
1 teaspoon ground cinnamon
3/4 cup vegetable oil
3 eggs
1 cup buttermilk
1 cup prune puree (can use baby food)

GLAZE:
1 cup sugar
1/2 cup buttermilk
1 teaspoon vanilla extract
1 tablespoon light corn syrup
1/2 cup (1 stick) butter

Preheat oven to 325 degrees. Grease and flour a 9-by-12-inch baking dish. Sift dry ingredients together, then stir in remaining ingredients in order given. Pour batter into prepared pan and bake for about 40 minutes. While pudding bakes, combine glaze ingredients and bring to a boil. Pour over pudding in pan while hot. (Note: This also bakes well in a traditional pudding mold. At serving time, soak sugar cubes in lemon or orange extract, place around pudding on small pieces of aluminum foil, and ignite.)

SERVES 10–12

When Dianne Hogerty's children were small, this recipe caught her eye because of "visions of sugarplums dancing in their heads." She fondly remembers carrying the flaming pudding into the darkened dining room and watching those little eyes light up.

Bananas Foster

1/4 cup (1/2 stick) butter
1/4 cup firmly packed brown sugar
1/4 teaspoon ground cinnamon
2 firm bananas, cut into 1/2-inch slices
1/2 cup dark rum
8 scoops vanilla ice cream

Melt butter, sugar, and cinnamon in a sauté pan. Add bananas and sauté until they begin to soften. Pour in rum, tilt pan slightly, and ignite liquor. Gently shake pan to prolong flames. When flames go out, spoon sauce and bananas over ice cream.

SERVES 4

There's no need to forgo any dessert-time drama when there are fewer revelers at the holiday table. This classic flaming dish originated in New Orleans, lending a rich serving of the South to any occasion.

Red Pears in Caramel Sauce

A *cloaking of caramel beautifully dresses up simple winter fruits. Amy Winn shared this enticing combination, a favorite from her friend Susan Miller in Dallas.*

2 red pears, halved and cored
2 tablespoons fresh lemon juice
1/4 cup fig preserves
Whipped cream

SAUCE:
1/4 cup (1/2 stick) butter
3/4 cup firmly packed brown sugar
1 cup heavy cream
1 tablespoon cognac

Preheat oven to 325 degrees. Place pear halves in enough water to cover, add lemon juice, and poach for about 4 to 5 minutes. Drain and place in a baking dish, cut-side up. Spoon 1 tablespoon fig preserves in the center of each pear. To make sauce, combine butter and brown sugar, and bring just to a boil. Remove from heat and whisk in heavy cream. Return to low heat and cook until thickened. Stir in cognac. Spoon sauce over pears in baking dish and bake for 30 minutes, basting every 10 minutes. Serve with sauce and whipped cream.

SERVES 4

Cranberry-Apple Tart

Another inviting vehicle for fresh seasonal fruit is the open-faced tart, such as this beauty from chef Sarah Garney. Scale your tarts to suit the occasion—they can be enjoyed at full size, individual size (sometimes called "tartlets"), or even bite size.

1 cup all-purpose flour
1/2 cup finely chopped pecans
1/4 cup sugar
1/4 cup (1/2 stick) butter, softened
1 egg
2-1/2 cups fresh whole cranberries
2 small Granny Smith apples, peeled and diced
1-1/2 tablespoons grated orange zest
3/4 cup firmly packed brown sugar
1/2 teaspoon ground cinnamon
Pinch of ground cloves

Combine flour, pecans, and sugar, then blend in butter and egg until mixture becomes crumbly. Press dough onto bottom and sides of a 10-inch tart pan. Cover and refrigerate for 1 hour. Preheat oven to 350 degrees. Combine remaining ingredients and spoon into chilled tart shell. Bake for 25 to 30 minutes, or until crust is golden and fruit is bubbly. Serve warm or at room temperature.

SERVES 6–8

Fragrant Baked Apples

4 baking apples, cored
1/2 cup firmly packed brown sugar
1 teaspoon ground cinnamon
1/4 teaspoon ground nutmeg
1/4 cup toasted slivered almonds
1/4 cup seedless raisins
1/4 cup Irish Mist liqueur
3/4 cup water
Juice of 1 lemon
1/4 teaspoon finely grated orange zest

Preheat oven to 350 degrees. Remove 1 inch of peel from top of each apple. Place apples in a baking dish. Mix brown sugar, cinnamon, nutmeg, almonds, and raisins, and fill center of each apple. Combine Irish Mist, water, lemon juice, and orange zest, and pour over apples. Bake for 35 to 40 minutes, or until apples are tender. Serve with sauce spooned over tops.

SERVES 4

Baked apples make soothing desserts during the fall and winter months. This version is packed with holiday goodies—spices, nuts, raisins, and a hint of orange, all against the warm background of Irish Mist.

Macadamia-Crusted Pear Torte

1-1/2 cups all-purpose flour
1/2 cup melted butter
1 cup sugar
1/2 cup chopped macadamia nuts
1 (8-ounce) package cream cheese, softened
1 egg
1 teaspoon vanilla extract
2 pears, peeled and sliced
1 teaspoon pumpkin pie spice
1 teaspoon fresh lemon juice

Preheat oven to 350 degrees. Combine flour, butter, 1/2 cup sugar, and nuts, and pat into an 8-inch springform pan (bottom and sides). Bake for 12 minutes or until beginning to brown. Set aside to cool. Increase oven temperature to 400 degrees. Combine cream cheese, 1/4 cup sugar, egg, and vanilla extract, and pour into crust. Toss fruit with spice, lemon juice, and remaining 1/4 cup sugar. Arrange pears in a circle on cream cheese filling and pour any sugared juice left from tossing fruit on top. Bake for 20 to 25 minutes.

SERVES 8–10

Buttery-rich, slightly sweet macadamia nuts form a delicious embrace for this torte's fruit and cheese filling. Try serving individual portions sprinkled with bits of crystallized ginger.

Brandied Chocolate Pie

This rich chocolate treat would be the perfect offering for coffee and dessert after attending "The Nutcracker." Jim and Georgia Lynch created it one year for the Gourmet Gala, and it's become their favorite Christmas Eve dessert ever since.

2 egg whites
1/8 teaspoon salt
1/8 teaspoon cream of tartar
1/2 cup sugar
1/2 cup chopped English walnuts
1/2 teaspoon vanilla extract
4 ounces sweet chocolate
3 tablespoons water
2 tablespoons brandy
1 cup heavy cream, whipped
Shaved chocolate

Preheat oven to 300 degrees, and lightly grease an 8-inch pie pan. Beat egg whites, salt, and cream of tartar until fluffy. Beat in sugar 2 tablespoons at a time. Continue beating until mixture forms stiff peaks. Gently fold in nuts and vanilla. Spoon into prepared pan and make a "nest," building sides up 1/2 inch above edge of pan but not over rim. Bake for 50 to 55 minutes, then set aside to cool. Combine chocolate and water over low heat, and stir until melted. Cool, then stir in brandy. Fold chocolate mixture into whipped cream, then spoon into shell. Chill for 2 hours. Garnish with shaved chocolate.

SERVES 6–8

Pumpkin Cream Pie

Donna Wilting shared this heavenly alternative to the usual heavy pumpkin pie. She and her sister Debbie Graham celebrate on Christmas morning with a brunch for their families and relatives, and this dessert always appears at these gatherings.

3/4 cup sugar
3 tablespoons cornstarch or 1/3 cup flour
1/2 teaspoon salt
1 teaspoon ground cinnamon
1/2 teaspoon ground nutmeg
1/2 teaspoon ground ginger
1/4 teaspoon ground cloves
1 cup canned pumpkin
2 cups milk
3 slightly beaten egg yolks
1 (9-inch) baked pie shell
1 cup heavy cream, whipped with 1 tablespoon sugar, 1 teaspoon
    vanilla, and 1/4 teaspoon ground cinnamon

Combine sugar, cornstarch, salt, and spices. Gradually stir in pumpkin and milk. Cook, stirring constantly, until mixture thickens and comes to a boil. Cook and stir for 2 minutes, then remove from heat. Stir a small amount of hot mixture into egg yolks, then stir yolks into hot mixture. Cook and stir for 2 minutes. Pour into a bowl and cover with waxed paper gently pressed on top of hot filling. Refrigerate for 2 to 3 hours. Mix half of whipped cream with pie filling and pour into cooled pastry shell. Top with remaining whipped cream.

SERVES 8

Ripples-of-Chocolate Cheesecake

1-1/2 cups Oreo cookie crumbs (about 30 cookies)
3 tablespoons butter or margarine, melted
1/2 cup semisweet chocolate chips
4 (8-ounce) packages cream cheese, softened
1-1/4 cups sugar
3 tablespoons cornstarch
1/4 teaspoon salt
5 large eggs
1 cup sour cream
2 teaspoons vanilla extract
1-1/2 cups heavy cream
8 ounces white chocolate
8 ounces semisweet chocolate

Preheat oven to 350 degrees, and grease a 9-inch springform pan. Combine cookie crumbs and butter, and press onto bottom of pan. Bake for 12 to 15 minutes, then remove from oven and sprinkle with chocolate chips. Let stand for several minutes, then spread softened chocolate evenly over crust. Refrigerate. Beat cream cheese at medium speed until light and fluffy. Combine sugar, cornstarch, and salt, and gradually beat into cream cheese until blended. On low speed, gradually beat in eggs, sour cream, vanilla, and 1 cup heavy cream until blended and smooth.

Divide batter evenly between two containers with pouring spouts. In separate pans over very low heat, melt white and semisweet chocolates. Stir melted dark chocolate into one container of batter and white chocolate into the other. Pour half of dark batter into springform pan, then, holding white batter about 2 feet above pan, pour about half of white batter into center of dark batter. Repeat step 3 times, alternating white and dark batters and decreasing amounts each time, ending with white batter (top of cake should look like a "bull's eye" target). Bake for 30 minutes, then reduce temperature to 325 degrees and bake for 1 hour and 45 minutes more, or until center is set. Turn off heat and let cheesecake sit in oven for 1 hour. Run a knife around edge to loosen, and cool in pan on wire rack. Refrigerate for at least 6 hours.

SERVES 12–14

Traditions are often launched unexpectedly. When cheesecake-lover Sheryl Koch made this one several years ago for a Christmas party at work, she had no idea she was about to create an annual stampede. She adapted her version from an award-winning cake by Arlene Schlotter.

Sparkling Truffle Cake

This flourless cake is actually one big truffle—a dessert that will make chocolate lovers swoon. Very little effort here produces very sophisticated results (a sort of Christmas present for the cook!).

8 ounces good-quality semisweet chocolate
1 cup sugar
1 cup unsalted butter
1/4 cup Grand Marnier liqueur
4 eggs
Confectioners' sugar
Silver bead sprinkles

Preheat oven to 350 degrees. Grease and line with foil an 8-inch springform pan. In a double boiler, melt chocolate with sugar and butter, then remove from heat. When cool, stir in liqueur and beat in eggs. Pour batter into prepared pan and bake for about 30 to 35 minutes, or until a crust forms on top. Cool to room temperature, then refrigerate overnight in pan. Remove from pan, dust top with confectioners' sugar (using a paper doily template if desired), and sprinkle with silver.

SERVES 10

Candied-Ginger Gingerbread

Gingerbread creations are definitely the province of the holidays, and not just in the form of men or houses. This peppery homespun cake is delicious served with a sauce made from ginger and fresh oranges (see p. 103).

1-1/2 cups all-purpose flour
1 teaspoon baking soda
1 teaspoon ground ginger
1 teaspoon ground cinnamon
1/2 teaspoon salt
1/2 teaspoon pepper
1/2 cup (1 stick) unsalted butter, softened
1/2 cup firmly packed brown sugar
2 eggs
1/4 cup dark molasses
2/3 cup buttermilk
1/4 cup chopped crystallized ginger

Preheat oven to 325 degrees. Grease and flour an 8-inch cake pan. Sift together flour, baking soda, spices, salt, and pepper. Beat butter until light and fluffy, then add sugar and beat until fluffy again. Add eggs 1 at a time, beating well after each addition, followed by molasses. Stir half of dry ingredients into mixture, then buttermilk, then remaining dry ingredients. Fold in crystallized ginger. Pour batter into prepared pan, and bake until a tester inserted comes out clean (about 45 minutes). Cool slightly in pan on a wire rack, then cut into squares and serve warm.

SERVES 8

Clove Cake with Caramel Frosting

3 cups sifted all-purpose flour
1 tablespoon ground cloves
1 tablespoon ground cinnamon
1 teaspoon baking powder
1/2 teaspoon baking soda
1/8 teaspoon salt
1 cup seedless raisins
1 cup (2 sticks) butter, softened
2-1/4 cups sugar
5 eggs
1 cup buttermilk

FROSTING:
1/2 cup (1 stick) butter or margarine
1 cup firmly packed brown sugar
1/3 cup light cream or evaporated milk
2 scant cups confectioners' sugar
1 teaspoon vanilla extract or 1/2 teaspoon maple extract

Preheat oven to 350 degrees. Lightly grease a 10-by-4-inch tube pan. Sift 2-3/4 cups flour with spices, baking powder, soda, and salt, and set aside. Toss raisins with remaining flour. At medium speed, beat butter until creamy, then gradually add sugar, beating until mixture is light and fluffy (about 5 minutes). In another bowl, beat eggs until light and fluffy, then blend into sugar mixture at medium speed, scraping down sides of bowl. At low speed, alternately add flour mixture and milk to sugar-egg mixture, beginning and ending with flour. Beat only until blended. Stir in floured raisins, then pour batter into prepared pan. Bake for 60 to 65 minutes, or until a tester inserted comes out clean. Cool in pan on a wire rack for 20 minutes. Gently loosen sides with a spatula, then turn cake out onto rack. Cool completely (about 1 hour) before frosting.

To make frosting, melt butter over low heat. Remove from heat and add brown sugar, stirring until smooth. Return to low heat and bring to a boil, stirring. Boil, stirring, for 1 minute, then remove from heat and add cream. Over low heat, return just to boiling again. Remove from heat and let cool to 110 degrees on a candy thermometer, or until bottom of saucepan feels lukewarm. At medium speed, beat in confectioners' sugar until mixture becomes thick (if too thin to spread, gradually add a little more sugar). Add vanilla. Set mixing bowl in a bowl of ice water, and beat until frosting is thick enough to spread and barely holds its shape. Spread on cooled cake.

SERVES 12–14

When Karen Adler reflects on her mother's kitchen during the holiday season, the memories swirl with pungent aromas and tastes. Her penchant for spiced goodies developed early and permanently there. Although the frosting for this cake may seem too laden with "steps," it's definitely worth every stroke.

Snowball Cake

Linda Yeates obtained the recipe for this special cake years ago from her former mother-in-law Effie, who called it "Miss Margaret's Cake." Surrounded by a garland of holly and wired brocade ribbon, this would be just the thing for a small holiday wedding.

1 cup (2 sticks) butter
2 cups sugar
3 cups all-purpose flour
1 teaspoon baking soda
1 teaspoon baking powder
1/2 teaspoon salt
1 cup buttermilk
6 egg whites
1 teaspoon vanilla extract

FILLING:
1/2 cup sugar
1 heaping tablespoon all-purpose flour
Pinch of salt
1-3/4 cups milk
6 egg yolks

FROSTING:
1/4 cup confectioners' sugar
2 cups heavy cream
1 cup flaked coconut

Preheat oven to 350 degrees. Grease and flour three 8-inch cake pans. Cream together butter and sugar. Combine flour, baking soda, baking powder, and salt. Add to butter mixture gradually, alternating with buttermilk. Beat egg whites until stiff, then fold into batter along with vanilla. Pour into prepared pans and bake for 25 minutes or until cake springs back from touch. Cool slightly in pans on wire racks, then remove from pans and continue cooling on racks.

To make filling, combine sugar, flour, and salt, then stir in milk. Heat over medium-low heat, then stir in egg yolks and continue cooking until mixture thickens. Remove from heat and cool completely. When cake is cool, spread cooled filling between layers, then onto sides and top. (Note: If necessary, keep layers in place with long toothpicks.)

To make frosting, combine sugar and cream, and beat on high speed until mixture is thick enough to peak. Spread on cooled cake and sprinkle top with coconut.

SERVES 16–20

Ice Box Fruitcake

4 cups chopped nuts
1 (15-ounce) package golden raisins
1/4 pound green candied cherries
1/4 pound red candied cherries
1/2 pound flaked coconut
1 pound graham crackers, crushed
1 (16-ounce) package miniature marshmallows
1 (5-ounce) can evaporated milk

Combine first 6 ingredients and set aside. Melt marshmallows with milk over a very low heat. Pour melted marshmallow mixture over nut-and-fruit mixture, and toss until mixture forms a large stiff ball. Pack mixture firmly (no air spaces) into a rectangular cardboard cracker box and refrigerate for at least 12 hours. Tear box away and slice cake into thin squares or triangles.

SERVES 16–20

Karen Zecy always thinks of this recipe at Christmas because it was so easy for her and her sister to prepare as children. Shelley Bradley shared a similar one from her mother-in-law Pauline, who rolled the dense treat and sliced it like cookies.

Dee's Fruitcake

1 cup Wesson oil (no substitution)
1-1/2 cups firmly packed brown sugar
4 eggs
3 cups all-purpose flour
1 teaspoon baking powder
2 teaspoons salt
2 teaspoons ground cinnamon
2 teaspoons ground allspice
1 teaspoon ground cloves
1 cup pineapple juice
2 cups mixed citron
1-1/2 cups candied cherries
1-1/2 cups whole dates
1 cup whole walnuts
2 cups whole mixed nuts

Preheat oven to 275 degrees and place a pan of water on lower rack. Grease two 9-by-5-inch loaf pans and line with brown paper. Combine oil, sugar, and eggs. In a separate bowl, combine 2 cups flour, baking powder, salt, and spices. Blend flour mixture into sugar-egg mixture, alternating with pineapple juice. Toss fruits and nuts with remaining 1 cup flour, and stir into batter. Pour mixture into prepared pans and bake for 2-1/2 to 3 hours. Cool thoroughly on wire racks before removing brown paper from bottom of cakes.

SERVES 20–30

If you're looking for Dee Conde during Christmastime, check the kitchen first. This very traditional fruitcake was an annual production when daughter Karen was growing up.

Black Walnut Apple Cake
with Calvados Sauce

The strong, slightly bitter flavor of black walnuts offers a tasty partner for apples and holiday spices. Take care not to underbake this dense, delicious cake, which is also very good without the sauce.

3 cups all-purpose flour
2 cups sugar
1 teaspoon baking soda
1 teaspoon ground cinnamon
1 teaspoon ground cloves
1 teaspoon salt
1-1/4 cups Wesson oil (no substitution)
3 eggs, beaten
2 teaspoons vanilla extract
5–6 tart apples, peeled and chopped
1 cup chopped black walnuts

SAUCE:
1/2 cup heavy cream
1/2 cup half-and-half
1/4 cup sugar
2 egg yolks
1/4 cup Calvados brandy

Preheat oven to 375 degrees. Combine flour, sugar, baking soda, spices, and salt. Stir in oil, eggs, and vanilla (mixture will be dense). Blend in apples and nuts. Pour batter into a 9-inch spring-form pan and bake for about 70 minutes, or until top of cake is crisp and dark golden brown (do not underbake.) Cool on a wire rack before removing sides of pan. To make sauce, combine cream and half-and-half, bring to a boil, and then set aside. Beat together sugar and eggs, then slowly add cream mixture, whisking to blend. Return to low heat and stir until mixture coats the back of a spoon. Let cool, then stir in brandy before serving over cake.

SERVES 8–10

Smooth Applesauce Cream

For apple lovers on the run, this no-bake dessert is quick and very appealing served in sherbet glasses or individual-size crusts. Although assembled right off the shelf, the floral echo of lemon zest freshens the taste quite a bit.

1 (15-ounce) jar sweetened applesauce
3/4 teaspoon ground cinnamon
3 tablespoons sugar
1-1/2 teaspoons minced fresh lemon zest
1 cup heavy cream, whipped
Toasted pecan pieces (optional)

Combine applesauce, cinnamon, sugar, and lemon zest. Gently fold in whipped cream. Chill well. Top with pecans and serve.

SERVES 6–8

Walnut-Eggnog Mousse

2 envelopes unflavored gelatin
1/2 cup cold water
4 cups commercial eggnog (dairy variety, not canned)
1/4 teaspoon ground nutmeg
2 tablespoons rum
1 cup chopped English walnuts

Soften gelatin in water, then add 1 cup eggnog and heat until gelatin dissolves. Remove from heat and add remaining eggnog, nutmeg, and rum. Chill until partially set, then whip until light and fluffy. Stir in walnuts, then refrigerate until ready to serve.

SERVES 8–10

Commercial eggnog usually begins appearing in grocers' dairy cases around mid-October, so there's no need to wait until Christmas proper to enjoy this lovely mousse. Although delicious unadorned, you may also want to try it with a raspberry sauce
(see p. 104).

Cold Lemon Mousse

1 envelope unflavored gelatin
1/4 cup cold water
3 eggs, separated
1 cup sugar
Juice and grated zest of 2 lemons
2 cups heavy cream
1 tablespoon confectioners' sugar
1 teaspoon vanilla extract

Stir gelatin into cold water and let soften. Beat egg yolks with sugar, then add lemon juice and zest. Beat egg whites until stiff and set aside. Whip cream with sugar and vanilla. Heat gelatin until dissolved, then fold into lemon mixture. Fold egg whites and 1-1/2 cups whipped cream into lemon mixture and chill. Spoon mousse into a glass bowl and top with remaining whipped cream.

SERVES 6–8

Cold, silky mousse as a light finale is just right after heavy holiday fixings. Stick a thin, crisp dessert wafer into the fluffy mound on each serving plate.

Pear and Raspberry Sorbet

This classy sorbet duo from Diana Phillips offers a nifty detour from traditional Yuletide chocolates and fruitcakes. Garnished with holly sprigs, this dessert beautifully displays the palette of the season.

PEAR SORBET:
1-1/2 pounds firm ripe Bosc or Bartlett pears, peeled, cored, and quartered
1 cup water
1/4 cup Sauterne wine
4 cardamom pods
Juice of 1/2 lemon
1 cup sugar

RASPBERRY SORBET:
1 pound raspberries (reserve some for garnish)
Juice of 1 lemon
1-1/4 cups sugar
1 cup water
Chilled vodka

Holly for garnish

Line a 9-by-5-inch loaf pan with plastic wrap. Combine pears, water, wine, cardamom, and lemon juice, and bring to boil. Cover and simmer over low heat for 10 minutes or until tender. Remove pears from liquid, allow to cool, and puree until smooth. Strain cooking liquid, pour into a fresh saucepan, and stir in sugar. Dissolve over low heat (do not stir), then bring to a boil and cook over high heat for 3 minutes. Remove from heat and let syrup cool completely.

Puree raspberries with lemon juice, strain to remove any seeds, and set aside. Dissolve sugar in water as above and set aside until cool. When both syrups are cool, stir pear puree into one and raspberry puree into the other. Pour into separate containers and freeze until firm, then beat well to break up ice crystals. Refreeze and repeat process 2 times. Spoon pear sorbet into prepared loaf pan, smooth the surface, and freeze until firm. Press raspberry sorbet on top of pear sorbet, smooth surface, and freeze again for several hours. To serve, remove from freezer and allow to soften for 10 to 20 minutes in the refrigerator. Turn sorbet out onto a cutting board, remove plastic wrap, and slice. Flood each serving plate with chilled vodka, place a slice of sorbet in the middle of each, and garnish with reserved raspberries and holly. Serve immediately.

SERVES 8–10

Rosy Cranberry-Port Sorbet

3 to 3-1/2 tablespoons sugar
2 tablespoons water
2 cups whole fresh cranberries
2 tablespoons Port wine

Combine sugar and water, and bring to a boil. Add cranberries, cover, and cook over medium-high heat, stirring occasionally, until berries pop and are tender (about 5 minutes). Stir vigorously to break cranberries into a pulp. Set aside to cool. Stir in wine, then cover and refrigerate for at least 1 hour. Pour mixture into an ice cream maker and process according to manufacturer's directions. (Note: Instead of Port, you can substitute Chambord liqueur, but use less sugar for this variation.)

SERVES 2–4

Versatile cranberries frequently show up as just "a face in the crowd" during the holidays, co-starring with nuts and other fruit in baked goods and relishes. Let them take center stage here, accepting a bow from a vintage Port. Substitute fruit juice if preferred.

Spicy Ginger Ice Cream

2-1/4 teaspoons ground ginger
1/4 teaspoon salt
1-1/4 cups sugar
2 cups milk
2 cups heavy cream
3 teaspoons vanilla extract

Combine ginger, salt, and sugar, add milk, and stir until sugar dissolves. Stir in cream and vanilla, then cover and refrigerate. Pour into an ice cream maker and process according to manufacturer's directions.

SERVES 10–12

Just a bit of spice turns basic vanilla ice cream into a treat fit for Good King Wenceslas. Try sprinkling servings of this creation with cocoa powder, shaved chocolate, or bits of candied ginger.

Yuletide Spirits

1/2 gallon vanilla ice cream, softened
3 jiggers brandy
1 jigger triple sec

Beat ingredients until smooth, then pour into serving bowls or glasses and freeze.

SERVES 12

Baked Alaska Peppermint Pie

1 (9-inch) deep-dish pie crust, baked and cooled
1 quart peppermint ice cream, softened

SAUCE:
2 tablespoons butter
1 cup sugar
2 ounces unsweetened chocolate
1 (6-ounce) can evaporated milk
1 teaspoon vanilla extract

MERINGUE:
3 egg whites
1/2 teaspoon vanilla extract
1/4 teaspoon cream of tartar
1/4 cup plus 2 tablespoons sugar

To make fudge sauce, combine butter, sugar, chocolate, and milk, and heat until thickened, stirring constantly. Add vanilla and remove from heat. Set aside to cool. Spread half the ice cream into prepared crust and cover with half the fudge sauce. Freeze until firm. Repeat process and freeze overnight. Before serving, prepare meringue topping. Preheat oven to 475 degrees. Beat egg whites with remaining ingredients until very stiff. Remove pie from freezer and spread with meringue mixture, sealing edges very well. Place in oven for just a few minutes, until meringue browns a little. Return pie to freezer and remove about 15 minutes before serving.

SERVES 10

Amaretto Caramel Cream

1 cup sugar
3/4 cup water
1 teaspoon vanilla extract
1 cup heavy cream or condensed skim milk
1/4 cup amaretto liqueur

Combine sugar, water, and vanilla in a heavy saucepan, and stir over low heat to dissolve sugar. Increase heat to medium-high and boil, without stirring, until mixture turns golden brown (about 5 to 10 minutes). Remove from heat and carefully whisk in cream. Return to low heat and stir until mixture thickens (about 5 minutes). Remove from heat and stir in amaretto.

MAKES 2-1/2 CUPS

Judith Fertig credits this lovely sauce to her mother and recommends enjoying it over poached pears, pound cake, or bread pudding.

Hot Fudge Sauce

6 tablespoons butter or margarine
2 cups sifted confectioners' sugar
2/3 cup cocoa
1 cup evaporated milk

Melt butter, add sugar and cocoa, and mix well. Add milk gradually, heating until smooth. Bring to a boil over medium heat and cook, stirring constantly, for about 5 minutes or until thick. (Note: Add 1 to 2 tablespoons of hot water if sauce is too thick.)

MAKES 2 CUPS

Marcia Hamilton also shared a "mom-made" holiday sauce. This one makes a much-appreciated gift, especially if you add walnuts.

Orange-Ginger Sauce

3 large oranges
1 cup plus 2 tablespoons orange juice
1/4 cup plus 2 tablespoons sugar
1 cinnamon stick
3 tablespoons chopped crystallized ginger

Peel oranges and remove membranes. Transfer segments to a bowl and set aside. Heat orange juice over low heat, then add sugar and cinnamon, stirring until sugar dissolves. Increase heat and simmer until mixture becomes syrupy and reduced to about 6 tablespoons (about 12 minutes). Remove cinnamon stick, pour liquid over oranges, and stir in ginger. Cool before serving.

MAKES ABOUT 1-1/2 CUPS

With its pieces of orange and candied ginger, this sauce creates a tasty garb for simple cakes, ice cream, or frozen yogurt.

Raspberry Cassis Sauce

Inspired by a sauce that JoAnn Dodson makes with amaretto, this cassis-laced version is wonderful spooned over heavy cake or fluffy mousse.

1 (10-ounce) bag frozen raspberries, thawed (reserve 1/4 cup juice)
1 tablespoon fresh lemon juice
1/2 cup sugar
2 tablespoons Crème de Cassis liqueur

Puree berries and juices, then strain and discard seeds. Transfer mixture to a saucepan and add sugar. Bring to a boil over medium heat, then reduce heat and simmer for 10 minutes. Stir in liqueur and refrigerate until serving.

MAKES ABOUT 1 CUP

Pineapple Dessert Sauce

This chunky fruit sauce pairs well with a variety of puddings, cakes, breads, and ice creams.

1 (6-ounce) can chopped pineapple
1/2 cup water
1/2 cup firmly packed brown sugar
Pinch of salt
1 tablespoon cornstarch
1/2 cup golden raisins
1/2 cup chopped pecans
2 tablespoons butter
1/4 cup dark rum

Drain juice from pineapple into a saucepan (reserve fruit). Add water, sugar, salt, and cornstarch, and stir over medium heat until mixture thickens. Add remaining ingredients and bring to a boil. Cool slightly before serving.

MAKES ABOUT 2 CUPS

Brown Sugar Hard Sauce

Serve this with a rich dense cake that's filled with nuts and spices, or prepare it as the traditional partner to festive plum pudding.

1 cup firmly packed dark brown sugar
1/2 cup (1 stick) unsalted butter
1 tablespoon hot water
1 tablespoon sherry
1 tablespoon brandy
1 teaspoon vanilla extract
Grated nutmeg

Cream butter and sugar until light and fluffy. Add water, sherry, brandy, and vanilla while beating continuously. Dust with nutmeg before serving.

MAKES 1-1/2 CUPS

DESSERTS

Sweet Treats

Truffles, Candy,
Cookies, & Bars

Tia Maria Truffles

1/2 cup sugar
1 cup whipping cream
8 ounces semisweet chocolate
2 tablespoons Tia Maria liqueur
1/2 cup chopped toasted almonds
1/2 cup confectioners' sugar

Heat sugar and whipping cream over medium heat. Remove from heat and stir in chocolate until melted, then add liqueur. Cover and freeze for 3 to 4 hours or overnight. Spoon out mixture and form into small balls. Roll half in almonds and half in sugar. Place in a covered container and refrigerate or freeze until ready to serve.

MAKES 5–6 DOZEN

Although simple enough to indulge in at any time of year, these decadent confections are perfect little "celebrations" for the holidays. Needless to say, anyone on your list would appreciate such a tasteful remembrance.

Mason's Famous Fudge

5 cups sugar
1-1/2 cups evaporated milk
18 ounces chocolate chips
6 ounces butterscotch chips
2/3 cup light or dark corn syrup
1/4 cup (1/2 stick) butter or margarine
2 teaspoons vanilla extract
1-1/2 cups chopped pecans or walnuts (optional)

Grease two 8-inch square baking pans or one 9-by-12-inch pan. Combine sugar and evaporated milk in a heavy saucepan, and cook over medium heat, stirring constantly, until mixture boils. Reduce heat to low and simmer for 10 minutes, stirring constantly, and scraping down crystallization on sides of saucepan. Remove from heat and quickly stir in chocolate and butterscotch chips, corn syrup, butter, and vanilla. Stir well until smooth and creamy. (Mixture gets stiff rapidly, so stir quickly with a heavy wooden spoon.) Add nuts and mix just until blended. As surface sets quickly, spread into pans promptly with rubber spatula. Chill for 1 to 2 hours, then cut into 1-inch squares.

MAKES OVER 100 SQUARES

Mason and Clara Skewis of Sheldon, Iowa, were very special friends of Jane Berkowitz from the time she was born. Well known for his fudge, Mason let the recipe evolve over the years until he hit on this one. Thankfully, Jane persuaded him to write it down.

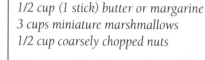

Easy Rocky Road Candy

Kelly Scanlon married a bona fide Rocky Road "nut," so her grandmother, Olla Belle Turchie, sends her every RR recipe she can find. This one adds a tasty touch to holiday trays.

2 cups semisweet chocolate chips
1/2 cup (1 stick) butter or margarine
3 cups miniature marshmallows
1/2 cup coarsely chopped nuts

Grease an 8-inch square pan. Place chocolate chips and butter in a large microwave-safe bowl and heat at 50% power for 5 to 7 minutes, or until chocolate has melted and mixture is smooth when stirred. Add marshmallows and nuts, blend well, and spread evenly into prepared pan. Cover and refrigerate until firm, then cut into 2-inch squares.

MAKES ABOUT 1-1/2 DOZEN

Microwave Peanut Brittle

Mary Ann Duckers confides that her dad's sweet tooth can't resist peanut brittle. This quick-and-easy version is one of his all-time favorites.

1 cup sugar
1/2 cup light corn syrup
1/8 teaspoon salt
1 cup raw peanuts
1 teaspoon butter
1 teaspoon vanilla extract
1 teaspoon baking soda

Combine sugar, corn syrup, salt, and peanuts in a glass bowl, and cook for 2 minutes on high (100% power). Stir, then cook on high for 8 minutes more, until mixture turns a light golden color. Add butter and vanilla, and cook 1 minute more on high. Stir in baking soda, and pour mixture onto a greased baking sheet. Working quickly, spread to desired thickness. Cool and break into pieces. Store covered.

MAKES ABOUT 2 DOZEN PIECES

Cookie Brittle

1 cup (2 sticks) butter or margarine, softened
1 cup sugar
1 teaspoon salt
1-1/2 teaspoons vanilla extract
2 cups all-purpose flour
1 cup chocolate chips
1 cup nuts (optional)

Preheat oven to 350 degrees. Combine butter, sugar, salt, and vanilla, and beat until creamy. Stir in flour gradually, beating until blended. Fold in chocolate chips and nuts, then press dough into a jelly-roll pan. Bake for 20 to 25 minutes (the shorter time it bakes, the chewier it stays; longer baking produces a crisper cookie). Leave in pan to cool, then break apart like peanut brittle. Store in an airtight container.

MAKES ABOUT 2 DOZEN PIECES

During the holidays Richie Cusick turns her house into a Christmas wonderland, ably assisted by spaniels Hannah and Meg (who raid candy bowls and remove stuffed mice from end tables, looking very busy). This recipe is one of the treats her guests enjoy each year.

Kris Kringle Sugar Cookies

3 cups all-purpose flour
1 teaspoon baking powder
1 teaspoon baking soda
1/4 teaspoon salt
1 cup (2 sticks) butter, chilled and cubed
2 eggs
1-1/2 cups sugar
1 teaspoon vanilla extract
1/2 teaspoon almond extract

Combine flour, baking powder, baking soda, and salt, mixing well with a pastry blender. Cut in butter until mixture crumbles. Beat eggs and add sugar slowly, followed by vanilla and almond extracts, continuing to beat until mixture is fluffy and light. Add to flour mixture, stirring by hand until dough forms. Wrap dough in waxed paper and refrigerate for about 1 hour. Preheat oven to 375 degrees. Using one-quarter of the dough at a time, roll out on a lightly floured surface. Cut out shapes using Christmas cookie cutters and place them 1 inch apart on ungreased baking sheets. Bake on the middle rack of the oven for 7 to 11 minutes, until edge of cookies turns golden. When cool, frost or decorate as desired.

MAKES 4–5 DOZEN

Baking sugar cookies with her children is one of the highlights of the season to Nancy McKay, ever since her young ones had to stand on chairs to reach the counter. Friend Donna Missimer remembers a similar production line in her mother's kitchen—make the dough one day, roll and cut the next, ice and decorate the following day.

Holiday Spritz Cookies

Rich, buttery spritz cookies are a traditional Scandinavian treat, and this version comes from Gayle Parnow. Add any candy decorations before baking the cookies.

1-1/2 cups (2-1/4 sticks) butter, softened
1 cup sugar
1 egg, well beaten
1 teaspoon vanilla or almond extract
Food coloring (optional)
3 cups sifted all-purpose flour
1 teaspoon baking powder

Preheat oven to 350 degrees. Cream butter and sugar with an electric mixer, then add beaten egg and vanilla. Beat until fluffy and light. If tinting dough, add food coloring at this point. Sift together flour and baking powder, then stir into creamed mixture. Place dough in a cookie press and press out desired shapes onto ungreased baking sheets. Bake for 7 to 8 minutes or until lightly browned.

MAKES ABOUT 6 DOZEN

Honey Nut Cookies

Jan Flanagan's grand-mother usually rolled up her sleeves in November or so to get these cookies going. One year she put two big batches on the attic stairs to age until Christmas, but then she forgot about them. Grandmommie next came across the tins in May when getting suitcases down for a cross-country trip. The family took the by-now vintage cookies in the car and pronounced them the best ever!

4 cups honey
4 cups milk
6 cups sugar
1 pound shelled almonds
4 ounces candied citron
4 ounces candied orange peel
4 ounces candied lemon peel
2 teaspoons ground cinnamon
1 teaspoon ground cloves
2-1/2 pounds all-purpose flour
2 heaping tablespoons baking soda
1 teaspoon salt

Combine honey, milk, and sugar, and boil for 15 minutes, then remove from heat. Combine almonds, candies, and spices in a large bowl, pour sugar mixture over, and stir well. Add as much flour as mixture will take, mixing well. Let cool, then add baking soda, salt, and remaining flour, and knead well. Let stand for at least 1 day. Preheat oven to 350 degrees. Roll out dough to 1/4-inch thick and cut into shapes with Christmas cutters. Bake on greased baking sheets for 15 to 20 minutes, until lightly browned. When cool, pack in containers and allow to age for several weeks to soften and mellow. (Note: Placing an apple slice in each container helps speed the softening.)

MAKES SEVERAL DOZEN

Rudolph's Nose Cookies

3/4 cup (1-1/2 sticks) butter or margarine, softened
3/4 cup sugar
1 egg plus 1 egg yolk
2 teaspoons almond extract
3/4 cup all-purpose flour
1/2 teaspoon baking soda
1/4 teaspoon salt
1 tablespoon water
15 candied red cherries, halved

Beat together butter, sugar, whole egg, and almond extract at medium speed until very light and fluffy. Combine flour, baking soda, and salt, then beat into butter mixture until well combined. Refrigerate, covered, for 1 hour. Preheat oven to 350 degrees. Using hands, form dough into 30 balls. Drop by teaspoonfuls onto ungreased baking sheets, 3 inches apart, and flatten by hand to 1/2-inch thickness. Slightly beat egg yolk and water, and brush mixture over cookie tops. Firmly press a cherry half in center of each cookie, then brush again with egg wash. Bake for 15 minutes, or until light gold in color. Cool cookies on a wire rack, then store in airtight containers.

MAKES 2-1/2 DOZEN

Kelly Scanlon shared this recipe with a note that it's the favorite Christmas cookie of her daughters Katie and Megan, particularly because they get to add the candied cherries.

Pecan Butterballs

2 cups all-purpose flour
1/2 teaspoon salt
1/2 cup chopped pecans
1 cup (2 sticks) butter, softened (no substitute)
1/2 cup sugar
1 teaspoon vanilla extract
1 teaspoon almond extract
Confectioners' sugar

Sift together flour and salt, then add pecans. Cream together butter and sugar until light and fluffy, then beat in vanilla and almond extracts. Slowly fold in flour-pecan mixture, 1/2 cup at a time, until just blended. Chill dough for 1 to 2 hours. Preheat oven to 325 degrees. Shape dough into 1-inch balls, handling quickly and lightly. Arrange 2 inches apart on ungreased baking sheets. Bake for 15 minutes, or until the color of pale sand. Cool cookies on a wire rack. When almost cool, roll in confectioners' sugar (do not roll in sugar when cookies are hot or sugar will melt and become gummy). Store in airtight containers.

MAKES 3–4 DOZEN

Food columnist Jane Berkowitz lost many of her favorite recipes in Kansas City's 1993 floods along Southwest Boulevard, but thankfully this one survived. It's a variation of one of the cookies her mother made when Jane was a wee one.

Snickerdoodles

This cookie smells heavenly as it bakes. Kelly Scanlon's husband Mike brought the recipe home from work one year, and it's become a melt-in-your-mouth holiday tradition at their house ever since.

1-1/2 cups (3 sticks) butter or margarine, softened
2 cups sugar
2 eggs
1/2 cup honey
4 cups all-purpose flour
1 teaspoon ground ginger
2 teaspoons ground cinnamon
1 tablespoon baking soda
1 teaspoon salt
Sugar-cinnamon topping (4 parts to 1 part)

Preheat oven to 375 degrees. Cream together butter and sugar, then beat in eggs and honey. Sift together flour, spices, baking soda, and salt, then add to egg mixture, mixing well. By the teaspoonful make small balls out of dough and roll in sugar-cinnamon mixture. Bake on ungreased baking sheets for 10 to 15 minutes.

MAKES ABOUT 4 DOZEN

Stained-Glass Cookies

Depending on the skill (and patience) of the baker, these pretty cookies can range from simple cutouts to more complicated designs. They make a delightful entry in a holiday cookie exchange— Cori Osborn's friend Anita brought a similar version to her "Cookies and Friends" party one year. Though fun and intriguing, it's best not to try these with kitchen helpers under age 10.

12 pieces (about 2 ounces) clear hard candies (such as Lifesavers)
1 (20-ounce) package refrigerated sugar cookie dough, chilled
1/4 cup flour, plus additional as needed

Preheat oven to 350 degrees. Line baking sheets with parchment. Place 3 or 4 candies of the same color in a plastic bag and seal. Using the smooth side of a meat mallet, gently pound to crush candies. Repeat with remaining candies, using several colors in all. Cut dough in half and return one half to refrigerator. Coat sides of remaining half with 2 tablespoons flour, then roll out to 1/8-inch thickness, using additional flour as needed to prevent sticking. Cut out shapes with a floured cookie cutter, then, with a smaller cookie cutter or a sharp knife, cut out the center of each shape, leaving a 1/2-inch frame. Gently brush excess flour from cookies and, using a spatula, place them 2 inches apart on prepared baking sheets. Place 1/4 to 1/2 teaspoon crushed candy in each cookie center, making sure candy touches edge of dough. Bake for 5 to 9 minutes, or until edges of cookies are light golden brown and candy has melted and filled centers. Cool on baking sheets until candy hardens, then transfer to wire racks to cool completely. Repeat with remaining dough and candies.

MAKES ABOUT 4 DOZEN

Milk Chocolate Florentines

2 cups uncooked quick oats
1 cup sugar
2/3 cup all-purpose flour
1/4 cup light corn syrup
1/4 cup milk
1 teaspoon vanilla extract
1/4 teaspoon salt
2/3 cup butter or margarine, melted
2 cups chocolate chips

Preheat oven to 375 degrees. Line baking sheets with foil. Stir oats, sugar, flour, corn syrup, milk, vanilla extract, and salt into melted butter and mix well. Drop by level teaspoonfuls about 3 inches apart onto prepared baking sheets. Spread thin with a rubber spatula. Bake for 5 to 7 minutes. Cool, then peel foil away from cookies. Melt chocolate chips in a double boiler over hot (not boiling) water, stirring until smooth. Spread chocolate on the flat side of half the cookies, then top with remaining cookies.

MAKES 3-1/2 DOZEN

Although the name suggests an Italian heritage, Austrian bakers actually get the credit for these chewy, candy-like cookies. This delicious version came from Donna Smithmier.

Melting Moments

1 cup (2 sticks) butter, softened
1/4 cup confectioners' sugar
2 cups all-purpose flour

FROSTING:
2 tablespoons butter
2 tablespoons confectioners' sugar, plus additional as needed
1 tablespoon boiling water
1/2 teaspoon vanilla extract
Food coloring (optional)

Cream together butter and sugar, then add flour and mix thoroughly. Refrigerate dough to chill slightly. Preheat oven to 350 degrees. Drop dough by half-teaspoonfuls and shape into balls in palm of hand. Arrange on baking sheets and flatten with a fork. Bake for 12 to 15 minutes or until light brown. To make frosting, cream together butter and 2 tablespoons sugar, then add boiling water, vanilla, and enough additional sugar to create spreading consistency. Tint frosting green or pink if desired. Spread frosting on flat side of half of cooled cookies, then top with remaining cookies.

MAKES 3–4 DOZEN

Brucie Hopkins credits her friend Marilyn Uppman as the originator of these wonderful treats. Try them with children of all ages—the results are fun and delectable.

Chocolate-Kiss Peanut Butter Cookies

Chocolate and peanut butter go together at the holidays like Donner and Blitzen. These companion flavors produce a tasty cookie here, one that looks like it's wearing an elf's peaked cap.

2-2/3 cups sifted all-purpose flour
2 teaspoons baking soda
1 teaspoon salt
1 cup (2 sticks) butter, softened
2/3 cup creamy peanut butter, room temperature
1 cup sugar, plus additional for rolling cookies
1 cup firmly packed brown sugar
2 eggs
2 teaspoons vanilla extract
60 chocolate "kisses" (foil removed)

Preheat oven to 375 degrees. Sift flour with baking soda and salt, then set aside. On medium speed, beat butter and peanut butter until well blended. Add sugars and beat until mixture is light and fluffy. Add eggs and vanilla, and continue beating until smooth. Stir in flour mixture until well combined. By level tablespoonful roll dough into 60 balls, then roll each in sugar. Place 2 inches apart on ungreased baking sheets and bake for 8 minutes. Remove from oven and press a chocolate "kiss" into top of each cookie. Return to oven and bake for 2 minutes more. Cool on wire racks.

MAKES 5 DOZEN

Cream Cheese Dainties

Dianne Morris always makes these "dainties" at Christmas because her neighbors and friends request them! The red and green cherries give them old-fashioned festive appeal on a china plate.

1/2 cup (1 stick) butter or margarine, softened
1 (3-ounce) package cream cheese, softened
1/2 cup sugar
1/4 teaspoon almond extract
1 cup sifted all-purpose flour
2 teaspoons baking powder
1/4 teaspoon salt
1-1/2 cups crisp rice cereal, crushed coarsely
Red and green candied cherry halves

Cream together butter, cream cheese, sugar, and almond extract until light and fluffy. Sift together flour, baking powder, and salt. Stir dry ingredients into butter mixture and mix only until well combined. Refrigerate mixture for 2 hours. Preheat oven to 350 degrees. Form dough into 1-inch balls, roll in crushed cereal, and arrange on ungreased baking sheets. Flatten slightly and top each with a cherry half. Bake for 12 to 15 minutes (cookies should not brown).

MAKES 3-1/2 DOZEN

Pan de Polvo

4 cups vegetable shortening
1-1/4 cups sugar
1/2 cup cold cinnamon tea
6 cups all-purpose flour
1/2 teaspoon ground cinnamon
1/2 envelope dry yeast

TOPPING:
2 cups sugar
2 cups confectioners' sugar
2 heaping teaspoons ground cinnamon

Preheat oven to 350 degrees. Cream together shortening, sugar, and cinnamon tea until smooth. Combine flour, cinnamon, and yeast, and add to creamed mixture. Drop dough by teaspoonfuls onto ungreased baking sheets, or roll out and cut with small cookie cutters and arrange on sheets. Bake for 10 to 12 minutes. Cool for 5 minutes, then roll in combined topping ingredients. Cover and store for 3 weeks until Christmas or other holiday occasion. (Note: Will keep for 6 months in a covered plastic container.)

MAKES 12–15 DOZEN

Kim Rodriguez shared this recipe from Natividad Vera, her grandmother who lives in Texas. For many generations the ranch families have made dozens of these cookies at a time, enough to last for the entire Christmas holiday season, since they did not go into town very often for groceries. These cookies traditionally are enjoyed after a dinner of wild game and pinto beans.

Perfect Gingersnaps

1-1/2 cups (3 sticks) butter or margarine, softened
2 cups sugar, plus additional for rolling cookies
2 eggs
1/2 cup molasses
4 cups all-purpose flour
1-1/2 teaspoons ground cinnamon
1-1/2 teaspoons ground cloves
3 teaspoons ground ginger
2 teaspoon baking soda
1/2 teaspoon salt

Preheat oven to 350 degrees. Cream butter and sugar, then blend in eggs and molasses. Sift together flour, spices, baking soda, and salt, and stir into creamed mixture, blending well. Form dough into small balls and roll in sugar. Arrange on ungreased baking sheets and bake for 8 to 10 minutes (balls will flatten out and tops will crack during baking).

MAKES 5–6 DOZEN

Ginger entertains in many guises over the holidays. The dough for these crisp goodies can be divided and frozen, ready for you to pull out and bake fresh in a snap.

Sour Cream Crescents

This recipe has become a regular player in Judith Fertig's Yuletide repertoire—it always gets rave reviews. These little pastries are great with dark, rich coffee or hot spiced cider.

1 cup (2 sticks) butter, cut into pieces and chilled
2 cups sifted all-purpose flour
1 egg yolk, beaten
1/2 cup sour cream
1/2 cup good-quality apricot or raspberry preserves
1/4 cup finely chopped pecans
1/2 cup flaked coconut
Sugar

With a pastry blender or two knives, cut butter into flour until mixture resembles fine crumbs. Combine egg yolk and sour cream, then blend into flour mixture. Form dough into a ball, then wrap and refrigerate for several hours or overnight. Preheat oven to 350 degrees. Divide dough into 4 portions, keeping each wrapped and refrigerated until ready to use. On a floured surface, roll each portion into a 10-inch circle. Spread 2 tablespoons of preserves over circle, followed by a sprinkling of 1 tablespoon pecans and 2 tablespoons coconut. Cut each circle into 12 wedges and, starting from the wide end, roll each wedge into a crescent and sprinkle with sugar. Arrange on ungreased baking sheets and bake for 20 minutes.

MAKES 4 DOZEN

Fruit & Berry Jam Bars

Dark, rich jams and jellies can easily dress up simple bars. The assorted flavors suggested here will produce pretty "jeweled" treats on a holiday tray.

1-3/4 cups all-purpose flour
2/3 cup sugar
1/2 teaspoon baking powder
3/4 cup (1-1/2 sticks) butter or margarine, softened
1 egg
2 teaspoons vanilla extract
1 teaspoon ground mace
Fruit and berry jams (assorted flavors)

Preheat oven to 350 degrees. Sift together flour, sugar, and baking powder. Combine butter, egg, vanilla, and mace, then add all at once to dry ingredients, mixing until dough forms. Divide dough into 4 pieces, then shape into rolls about 12 inches long and 3/4-inch wide. Place on 2 ungreased baking sheets, about 4 inches apart and 2 inches from edge of sheets. Using a knife handle, make a groove about 3/8-inch deep down the center of each dough strip. Fill the depression on each strip with a different flavor of jam. Bake for 15 to 20 minutes, or until lightly browned along the edges. While still warm, cut into 1-inch diagonal bars. Cool on wire racks.

MAKES 4 DOZEN

Treasure Bars

1/3 cup (5-1/3 tablespoons) margarine, softened
1/2 cup sugar
1/2 cup firmly packed brown sugar
1 egg
1 teaspoon vanilla extract
2 tablespoons water
1 cup all-purpose flour
1-1/4 teaspoons baking powder
1/4 teaspoon salt
1/2 cup flaked coconut
1/2 cup chopped walnuts
1 cup semisweet chocolate chips

Preheat oven to 350 degrees. Grease a 9-inch square baking pan. Cream margarine and sugars together, then add egg and mix well. Add vanilla and water, continuing to cream until mixture becomes light and fluffy. Sift together flour, baking powder, and salt, add to creamed mixture, and blend well. Stir in coconut, chocolate chips, and nuts. Press mixture into prepared pan and bake for 20 to 25 minutes. Cool and cut into 1-1/2-inch squares.

MAKES 3 DOZEN

One bite of these chunky bars from Deborah Reffitt and you'll stop wondering where the name came from. These delicious treats won a blue ribbon at the Polk County Fair, and they're just right alongside a cup of coffee or a bowl of ice cream.

Poppy Seed–Coconut Bars

1-1/2 cups all-purpose flour
1/4 teaspoon salt
1/4 teaspoon baking soda
1-1/4 cups sugar
1/2 cup (1 stick) butter or margarine, melted
1/3 cup honey
1/2 teaspoon almond extract
1-1/2 teaspoons vanilla extract
4 egg whites
2 tablespoons milk
1 cup flaked coconut
1/3 cup poppy seeds

Preheat oven to 350 degrees. Grease two 9-inch square baking pans and line with waxed paper. Sift together flour, salt, baking soda, and sugar. Add melted butter, honey, flavor extracts, egg whites, and milk, mixing well. Stir in coconut and poppy seeds. Pour batter into prepared pans and bake for 30 minutes, or until top is firm when pressed lightly. Turn out onto wire racks and remove waxed paper immediately. When cool, cut into bars.

MAKES ABOUT 3 DOZEN

The crunchy texture and nutty taste of poppy seeds create an amiable partner for sweet, chewy coconut. Offer these bars for dessert or with a strong cup of afternoon tea.

Traditional Shortbread

Shortbread was once associated exclusively with Christmas and Scottish New Year's, though now it's enjoyed year-round (and not just in the Highlands!). The traditional method involves a shallow round mold, but nowadays simple squares are more common.

1 cup (2 sticks) butter, softened
1/2 cup sugar
2 cups all-purpose flour

Preheat oven to 350 degrees. Cream together butter and sugar, then mix in flour. Work dough by hand for a few minutes, then pat into an ungreased 9-inch square pan. Smooth surface of dough with the bottom of a glass. Bake for about 30 minutes, or until golden brown. Cut into squares while still hot, then let cool before removing from pan.

MAKES ABOUT 1-1/2 DOZEN

Oatmeal Date Squares

Because "gooey" is this bar's middle name, wrap the squares in red or green foil before storing them in holiday containers. As an alternative to the date filling, fix these sometimes with mincemeat instead (2 cups will do).

8 ounces pitted chopped dates
1/2 cup sugar
1 cup water
1/4 cup fresh lemon juice
1/2 cup chopped walnuts
3/4 cup (1-1/2 sticks) butter, softened
1 cup firmly packed light brown sugar
1-1/2 cups all-purpose flour
1/2 teaspoon salt
1/2 teaspoon baking soda
1-1/2 cups uncooked oats

Preheat oven to 350 degrees. Grease a 9-by-12-inch baking pan. Combine dates, sugar, and water, and cook over medium heat, stirring, until thickened. Add lemon juice and walnuts, then set aside to cool. Beat butter and sugar until light and fluffy. Sift together flour, salt, and baking soda, then add to butter mixture along with oats. Mix together with hands until well combined. Press half of oat mixture into prepared pan, spread with date filling, then cover with remaining oat mixture and press lightly with hands. Bake for 25 to 30 minutes or until golden. Cool slightly and cut into bars while still warm.

MAKES ABOUT 3 DOZEN

Index

About the Authors

Karen Adler's publishing companies, Two Lane Press and Pig Out Publications, produce award-winning regional travel guides and cookbooks, including the *Cuisine Series, Stein's Day Trips,* and numerous barbecuing and grilling titles. Karen is a charter member of the Heart of America Chapter of the American Institute of Wine and Food, and a member of the International Association of Culinary Professionals. An accomplished gourmet cook, she has appeared often in televised cooking demonstrations on area stations.

Jane Doyle Guthrie is a nonfiction editor and book production consultant with a specialty in cookbook editing and development. Alongside editions for the trade, she frequently is involved in producing high-quality fund-raising cookbooks for organizations such as the National Kidney Foundation. In such a capacity Jane co-chaired the development of the award-winning *Above & Beyond Parsley* for the Junior League of Kansas City, Missouri. Though her cooking interests are varied, Jane particularly enjoys experimenting with fresh herbs.

Both authors make their home in Kansas City and currently are at work on new cookbooks and travel guides.

Order Form

ORDER DIRECT! Kansas City customers call 531-3119; long distance customers call (800) 877-3119. Faxes also welcome: (816) 531-6113.

Please rush the following book(s) to me:

___ copy(s) **A KANSAS CITY CHRISTMAS COOKBOOK** for $14.95 plus $3 shipping

___ copy(s) **SAN ANTONIO CUISINE** for $14.95 plus $3 shipping

___ copy(s) **DALLAS CUISINE** for $14.95 plus $3 shipping

___ copy(s) **SAN DIEGO CUISINE** for $12.95 plus $3 shipping

___ copy(s) **NASHVILLE CUISINE** for $12.95 plus $3 shipping

___ copy(s) **MEMPHIS CUISINE** for $12.95 plus $3 shipping

___ copy(s) **KANSAS CITY CUISINE** for $12.95 plus $3 shipping

___ copy(s) **BRANSON COOKIN' COUNTRY** for $9.95 plus $3 shipping

___ copy(s) **PURE PRAIRIE: RECIPES FROM THE HEARTLAND** for $14.95 plus $3 shipping

___ copy(s) **DAY TRIPS FROM KANSAS CITY** for $9.95 plus $3 shipping

___ copy(s) **DAY TRIPS FROM NASHVILLE** for $9.95 plus $3 shipping

___ copy(s) **DAY TRIPS FROM SAN ANTONIO AND AUSTIN** for $10.95 plus $3 shipping

METHOD OF PAYMENT

___ Enclosed is my check for $_____ (payable to Two Lane Press, Inc.)

___ Please charge to my credit card: ___ VISA ___ MasterCard

Acct. # _____

Signature _____

SHIP TO:_____ GIFT/SHIP TO:_____

_____ _____

_____ _____

_____ _____

_____ FROM:_____

MAIL COMPLETED ORDER FORM TO:

Two Lane Press * 4245 Walnut Street * Kansas City, MO 64111